THE
TUNNEL OF LIFE

*As seen through the eyes of
an eighty-five year old man*

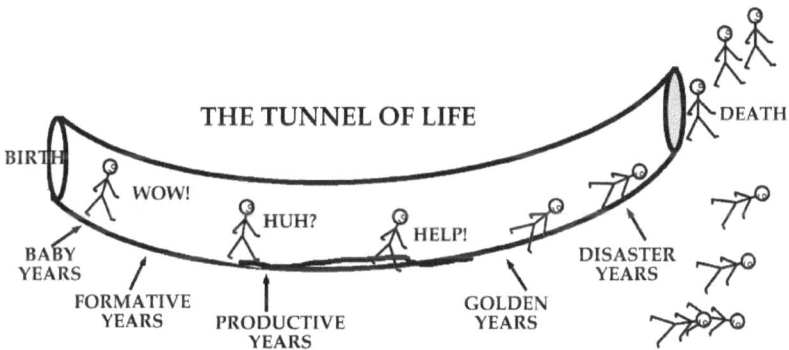

THE TUNNEL OF LIFE

BIRTH · WOW! · HUH? · HELP! · DEATH

BABY YEARS · FORMATIVE YEARS · PRODUCTIVE YEARS · GOLDEN YEARS · DISASTER YEARS

Lyle N. DeVine

The Tunnel of Life
By Lyle N. DeVine

Published by
Solutions Press
4533 MacArthur Blvd., #200
Newport Beach, CA 92660

First Edition August 2015
Printed in the United States

ISBN: 978-0-9846872-1-3

Contents

Acknowledgements

I would like to give a special thanks to Susan Carlson, Writer - Copyeditor, for her very professional efforts in helping me put this book together. Her guidance and expertise were instrumental in giving clarity to the book.

Also, I am deeply indebted to all those who wrote stories for this book, including the following friends and family members: Aaron, Alan, Alyssa, Brian, Bill, Charles, Cori, Christine, Carolyn, Dawn, Donald, Debra, Eddie, Elennor, Fred, Gary, Helen, Harold, Joan, Judith, Judy, John, Jeannine, Kevin, Kent and Colleen, Linda, Loren, Luther, Michael, Mac, Melva, Mike, Pamela, Qun, Ray, Sarah, Taylor, Tim, and Troy.

With much appreciation,

Lyle DeVine

Foreword

The TUNNEL OF LIFE is a story or recapitulation of any one person's life. You have to walk every step of your personal Tunnel of Life alone from birth to death.

Outside Influences - There are three outside influences that I can think of that affect anyone's Tunnel of Life.

The **First** outside influence is that once you are born, you are part of a family. You are stuck with your parents, good or bad. If they are a good influence, you will start making good decisions; but, if they dump you in a garbage bin, their Tunnel of Life has already closed in on them with poor decisions. However, this might be the best thing that could happen to you because whoever finds you will be a better influence on your life than if your parents had kept you.

The **Second** outside influence is if you are born with a mental or physical affliction that prevents you from having control over your Tunnel of Life.

The **Third** outside influence is if and when you decide to allow a moral equivalence to be a part of your life.

You cannot escape your Tunnel of Life: you live by your everyday decisions and those are governed by who and what you let into your Tunnel of Life. If you are not happy with life, only you can change it.

Later in this book you will find a story I wrote called "This is the First Day in the Rest of Your Life". Your Tunnel of Life is one personal decision after another. It's your Tunnel!

Five Stages - For the purpose of this book, I've given the Tunnel of Life five stages which we all go through, if we live long enough.

First is the "BABY YEARS". This is a time when your parents (mostly your mother) give you your first training in attitude, life, compassion, humor, and other life attributes that set the foundation for your future life. Your mother IS the most formative influence at this time.

The **Second** stage is the "FORMATIVE YEARS". These encompass all of the educational period of a person's life and may overlap the remaining stages. This is a very enchanting time of life.

The **Third** period or stage in the tunnel of life is the "PRODUCTIVE YEARS". These years are filled with all the complexities and excitements of the biggest portion of your life. What are You doing with Your Life?

The **Fourth** period or stage is the "GOLDEN YEARS". Some people feel these years are not all that *golden*, but they are usually a time when you do all those things you never got around to or didn't have time to do earlier in life.

Finally, there is the **Fifth** stage, the "DISASTER YEARS", which can be all that the phrase implies, but does not need to be.

This is a book about people's little excerpts of their lives. I hope their stories will help thousands of young people get a better start in life and head in a meaningful direction. Some of these stories are humorous and some are shocking, but none of them are boring or pointless.

Disclaimer: Some of the factual material in this book has had at least some research done on it and other stories more, but in my late age, I may not recall everything with complete accuracy. But, it is all true to the best of my knowledge and ability, so although I presume that not all people will agree entirely with what I have written; rest assured, it was not meant to be misrepresented or misinterpreted. It was meant to advise, inform, and be of educational value to any extent it could and should be.

Introduction

It was early fall of 2006 when my wife Bonnie and I purchased a nice three bedroom brick home in Longmont, Colorado. We had fallen in love with the kitchen and small patio just off the kitchen. We had never had a house with a basement before and it had lots of room. Like all the places we lived in, I started remodeling right way. Bonnie couldn't do stairs very well with her knee problems and her cardiomyopathy, so I opened up the wall between the kitchen and the garage and put in a double door closet for the washer and dryer which had been in the basement. We added air conditioning, an electronic air filtration system, and re-did the back yard with wrought iron fencing on both sides. For two years we polished the place until it was just the way we wanted it. We were very happy there, even with the winter weather; however, older people should never live in high altitude areas – they all go around with oxygen tanks if they have the slightest physical problems. We also had a situation come up with our youngest son. He worked for one of the largest corporations in the U.S. as a financial analyst. He was having three to four migraine headaches a week. The acetaminophen he was taking eventually damaged his liver to the extent that it became life-threatening.

We were considering moving back to California so we could keep an eye on him and he could do the same for us. It was late in December, 2008, just before Christmas, one night around 11 pm. Bonnie and I were playing cards in the kitchen, which we often did before bedtime, when I started to breathe heavily. I thought I had indigestion. I got up and walked toward the dining room to stretch, but soon I was on my hands and knees and finally rolling around on the floor trying to get air. It felt like an elephant was sitting on my chest. Bonnie saw I was in trouble and asked if I could make it to the car. I said "No, call an ambulance." At some point I passed out. I was aware that I had regained consciousness because Bonnie said, "You wet your pants." At this point, the ambulance arrived and the EMTs came in, checked me over, and gave me two aspirin. I asked for water, but they said "No. Chew them up." They put me on the gurney and off we went to the ambulance. There had been a lot of snow and it was very cold. I remember being put in the ambulance and they took forever doing "stuff". I said, "Close the damn door, I'm freezing to death." I don't remember anything beyond that until I woke up in intensive care. I was told that Dr. Stathis had just finished with his fourth heart attack patient when they rolled me in about midnight. At times I feel sorry for doctors; their days are never ending.

Lying there in intensive care, the thought of how fragile life is went through my mind. That was the moment I decided to write a book about life. I've never taken on this type of project before. The urge was overwhelming; it had to be done. At first I wanted the book to be about other people's lives, not mine. Then I decided it would be twice the book if it were stories that would help teenagers get started in a meaningful direction with their lives. This was because I knew what I wanted to do when I was a junior in high school. I ran the projectors in my home town's movie theater when I was in high school. The Principal, Mr. C.A. Williams, let me schedule a study hall period first thing in the morning, because I never got to bed before1 am.

I was lying in bed one morning reading some of the literature that colleges, institutes, and universities sent out to prospective students. Dunwoody Industrial Institute sent just the right information or stuff to me. It was the pivotal moment in my life. I thought...*we have an ice box in the kitchen, which mom's good friends gave to us when they got a new refrigerator.* Hardly anyone I knew had a refrigerator. Refrigerators and cooling systems were just coming into being, and I believed they would be great in the future. This is when I decided to get into the refrigeration and air conditioning business.

I never looked back from that moment. I finished high school and joined the Army (WWII was just ending and you either joined or got drafted). I finished my military service in Korea and headed for Dunwoody Industrial Institute in Minneapolis, MN. After Dunwoody, my life was on track for all time.

The writing of this book, which I dedicate to teenagers, is because (at the time of this writing) more than one third of all students entering high school in some parts of this country never reach graduation. Those who do finish often don't know what they plan to do, even after attending and finishing college.

By the way, the outcome of the large numbers of students who fail to complete high school does not speak well for parents or society. This is the "dumbing down of a nation". There should be more incentive created and instilled in our young people, not "junk" them. I recently read that many colleges make it easy for students from outside the state or maybe the country, to acquire entrance to those colleges because those colleges can make more money that way.

One of the most disgusting comments I ever heard was from Hillary Rodham Clinton, "*It takes a village to raise a child.*" This is Socialism and so untrue. It takes parents teaching their child everything they can about the aspects of life – including proper manners, respect, attitudes, compassion, and humor – before they ever reach public school. Babies see, hear, and react to everything around them. A goodly amount of education is in the next five to seven years of a child's life. Parents that interact with their babies in a positive way will turn out children (teenagers, and adults) who are well-groomed physically, intellectually, and spiritually, and possess great personalities, ideals, and enterprise.

Chapter One

The Baby Years

It all begins with a fetus becoming aware it is what it is. Yeah, hey, this is fun, just slopping around in warm water, not a care in the world. But, life goes on, and it can't stay this good forever. Soon trouble happens, all at once the water drains out and you are sitting in a sticky mess.

Then something seems to be pushing you in one direction... Yeah, that Old Man Time in the Tunnel of Life. It only goes in one direction. You say *"Wait a minute. I like it the way it was."* But it keeps pushing you towards that little round hole. *"It's too small, I can't get through there."* But life goes on; you crash into the hole and finally with great pain manage to squeeze through. They grab you by your feet, hold you upside down and spank you. You say *"What did I do wrong?"* You say *"Oh I know, these are first time parents, they do everything wrong."* You start to squeal and cry; they come running, wipe you off, wrap you in a warm blanket, and put you beside a warm body. *"Hey, this is nice"* so you go to sleep only to wake up too soon and your mother has not recovered enough to handle this, but that's what kids do – they learn to get *even* early. You wake up and find a strange new feeling, *"Yeah, I'm hungry"* so you scream like before and they come running again, jam a nipple in your mouth, it tastes good, and when you are full you fall off to sleep again. But life goes on; you wake up and find a new urge, so you subconsciously relieve yourself and it feels good and warm. Soon, however, it turns to irritation, so you scream and cry like a banshee. They come running and clean you up again. You scream because that's the only thing you know how to do and you get whatever you want when you do it.

Life goes on and pretty soon you find your hands and feet, and before long, you are crawling around. *"Man, this tunnel of life is big – it goes everywhere."* With enough eating, sleeping, and grunting, you develop more, can stand up and chase around. *"Yeah, this tunnel of life is huge."* Now is when you find out that you are not exactly alone in this world; there are others like you investigating this place, and sooner or later it happens – someone slugs you. *"Hey, that hurt!"* Now you can scream and cry or maybe just get even, so you slug back and all hell breaks loose until they come running again to fix everything. At this point in a child's life, we have to make a serious parental adjustment to the child's thinking. If parents don't take control of their children at this point in their life, childhood tantrums will most certainly become major fits of temper (probably in the Formative Years) resulting in the parent, teenager or young adult ending up in jail – for abuse, murder, rape, or whatever. Our lousy judicial system and human services divisions as they are today are so sadly lacking. There is a space the size of a football field, not a fine line, between correcting a child and abuse. Don't tell this to a lawyer though – he does not want to hear it. But that is another story. Let's get back to the Tunnel of Life.

The months during which a mother-to-be is pregnant, plus the next five years of the baby's life, are the most important years to determine the potential status of the baby's life. They are the precursor of how the baby's life will develop. If during pregnancy the mother drinks and smokes on a regular basis, or uses drugs, more than likely the child will be a slow learner at best.

A child needs its mother to be a best friend for those first years: to cuddle with, to read with, to draw love and compassion, and from whom to acquire a sense of well-being. Without this guidance a child will most likely not do well in school, and will not achieve the potential he or she should or could have. The teaching and guidance a child gets before entering any kind of school is the threshold to success. The Baby Years are short and most parents would say these precious years go by too fast. But this is the life of the Baby's generation, not the parents. The child only knows what it sees, feels and hears – curiosity is the norm at this age.

Parents often do not take the time to really enjoy their children. Children have their own logic and it shows in their actions. They check out a cat (tail first); or pull the petals off a flower. They have a perfect complexion that makes you just sit and look at them with envy. Everything children do is with complete sincerity: that's what makes them so perfect and beautiful. These precious moments and years go by so quickly that parents need reminding to grab them. That is one reason why I had to write this book.

Soon they enter the second stage of life – the Formative Years – and say goodbye to some of the most confusing years of their life.

A great lady shared this humorous story with me about her three-year-old daughter. One morning she asked her daughter what she wanted for breakfast. Her daughter Judy thought for a moment and said, "*I want the bread with the noise on top.*" It was toast – just a little child's logic.

Some years ago, one of my nieces was in a restaurant with her husband and two sons, ages four and six. Colleen is nearly total Irish, so her children have very fair complexions with the proverbial freckles. The waitress came to their table and seeing the boys so fair, she said, "*You boys must have been out in the rain.*" They said, "*No, we haven't.*" And the waitress said, "*You must have been; you have rust all over your faces.*"

Another time, Colleen told me about a situation her son and daughter-in-law had. It was Christmas-time and they were shopping with their young daughter Alexis. She said, "*Mommy, why are Santa's eyes blue at the mall, but at the church they are brown?*" There goes more of that child logic again. Parents do have their problems explaining.

PARENTS SOMETIMES DON'T GET IT RIGHT

Eddie was a teacher, but that didn't seem to fill the bill. Eddie decided to give his eight-year-old daughter a camera.

Well, she was trying to take pictures of her parents in the house in poor lighting. Eddie proceeded to explain to her that she would have to take pictures outside where there was more light. The next thing Eddie discovered was his daughter outside tapping on the window and shooting pictures of them through the window. Children do sometimes follow their parents' advice.

SOMETIMES PARENTS SHOULD THINK TWICE

This is a story from a realtor we had in Colorado. Joan and her son lived in an area that had a large open space between their tract and the next. There was a large berm or rise in the land behind their home and a young teenager was using the area as a shortcut with his car instead of going around on the street. This was stirring up a lot of dust and Joan was complaining about it in hearing distance of her very young son. She said, *"I wish someone would trap that guy."* As it went, her son dug a hole just over the berm and the teenager's car wheel got hung up in the hole. Joan's son said, *"Look, Mommy, I trapped the guy."* Joan said, *"You're going to be an engineer just like your father."* The teenager never drove there again.

The Tunnel of Life

Chapter Two

The Formative Years

The tunnel of life expands even larger - the child begins to use all of its God-given faculties that will control the destiny of its entire life: compassion, logic, love, hate, satisfaction, humor, beliefs, likes, dislikes, needs and direction. These are the years where your personality, integrity and your very self-being are initiated.

You, who were the child, are becoming an individual by character. You're beginning to establish your life's memories. You have an accomplished past. These are very personal and complicated years and are forerunners to your future's sum total.

A couple of reasons for a young person's well-being and accomplishments in these years are their diet, and the driving force of parents and teachers, or lack thereof. It would seem that fifty or sixty years ago, these forces were in better shape than they are today, thanks to a decline in Christianity, and too much lawyer intrusion. These are the years when you start to develop life-long friendships. But life goes on, you subconsciously say goodbye to all those years of training. Growing up, school, college, and whatever drive you instilled in yourself will start to show in how far you will push yourself from now on down the tunnel of life. One thing is for sure, it goes up hill all the way with just enough light to continue on. At this point in life I guess you get the idea – you know it all, can solve anything, and can take on all comers.

Life has its pitfalls - you are walking along in the tunnel of life and it seems to go uphill always, but sometimes it dips; you are wading through murky waters and it's not too clear up ahead; you're afraid something will jump out and bite you, but you go on to reach the other bank. You don't always have a handle on life's experiences, so you just wing it (so to speak) and hope for the best. This is much better than worrying: worry never solved anything and there is a difference between worry and concern. The Formative Years have their problems at times, but that's because these are the learning years and they are logically filled with mistakes. That is part of learning, just like despair and rejection. The Formative Years may seem hard and they are, but one thing is for sure, this is a time when you develop memories you carry through life to the very end. These years are notable ones, because this is the time when your life mold is made, your personal self-being and future existence is set in place, your love of life and future direction becomes indelible in your mind. These Formative

Years are different from the rest of your life – set apart in meaning and scope by their very nature and how they develop.

I believe I have been writing this book for years and didn't know it. Raised by my Mother alone (no Dad), I was instilled with her saintly philosophy. When I was young, I did my share of foolish things, but eventually my Mother's influence took control and I grew up in many ways. For the most part, I lived with Jesus Christ in my hip pocket. When it came to reacting to a situation, I didn't even have to make up my mind – it was already done. And when I looked at my children it was all there. Your Formative Years make you what you are, and it's easy to build on that, but impossible to start them at zero. Bad parents, lazy teachers, and loose laws can have an ill effect on young people.

To me humanity starts with the child. That just makes good sense. Life starts as a child, and as the child grows, it discovers, learns to think, and arrives at conclusions. These conclusions become a way of life, a code of ethics. All that is needed for success is to add God's faithfulness to the mix to produce a life of serene happiness. If a parent gives a child or young adult the parental incentive to do their best (and that *is* all the parent can do), it will be enough. They cannot be something they are not. The young adult will find the direction they feel is right, whether it be doctor, lawyer, or Indian chief. A young person has all those years ahead of them and they have to do something with those years. They might just as well make them count for something. God didn't put them on this earth and give them their faculties for nothing. I believe that we are meant to cut a swath in life of our own nature. We are all individuals, but we make and develop our own purpose.

Life really should be about memories, and to get them, you have to live your life out, not do some foolish thing that prevents you from ever getting there. Before you act or do something new or unusual, stop and think about it. It's your life. Guidance or advice is not always available. You can figure it out for yourself if you only use half of the intuition you were born with. I am sure that at least a few more people would live to see the Golden Years of old age. To be successful a person needs three basic precepts. First, you need to know through education what you are talking about or doing; Second, you have to have a decent attitude (you can be the smartest person in the world but with a lousy attitude people will stay away from you); and Third, you should have good moral and ethical standards. With these qualities, you will have a life worth living.

In trying to put together all the complicated facts of life as we know them today, I find myself going back more and more to the younger years. This only makes good sense, because what you do in early life has a great bearing on the rest of your life and your life expectancy. For example, years ago people (possibly in their Productive Years or later) feeling dissatisfied with themselves, or finding that life and success were not going their way, would turn to drinking and the more they drank, the sooner they did themselves in. Today, with all the drugs available, young people are finding themselves in the same situation, but it is a far more daunting addiction. They are too young to maneuver their way through the drug world alone, and their lives are all too often cut short or ruined. If we do not close down our southern borders, it will only get worse. You have to realize there is an entirely different world in Mexico than what we have here in the United States. Furthermore, Washington is politically broken, because if the majority of the citizens in these United States wish for a specific situation to become law, Congress will most certainly vote the other way time and time again. With special interest groups at work, it doesn't make a whole lot of difference which party is in control. Each has their own reasons for screwing up, and, in general, they seem to be nefarious, mendacious, obnoxious, devious, and have the most ludicrous and clandestine reasons for what they do. Those who are in power at the present (2010) are using Saul Alinsky's (*Rules for Radicals*) philosophy – "Destroy your enemies; Accuse them of what you are doing; and All power is in the hands of the government". We are living in a state of Constitutional decadence.

One of the most important pieces of advice that I can give to anybody is one I learned in high school from a teacher who only lectured. It is something that I've found some people never learn in a lifetime and it can take a terrible toll on a person's life. It is "to **always** separate fact from fiction". Every advertisement out there tells you "how wonderful a product is", or "it is the best one there is." These statements tell you nothing about the product, and they always tell you to "Call Now!" at the end of their spiel. Another thing being promoted is "Buy the extended warranty." For today's products the warranties usually are not worth the paper on which they are written, because the product outlives the warranty. Another piece of advice – when you hear that knock on the door and it is someone you don't know (usually in the evening or at an off-time) - whatever they are promoting is more than likely a scheme or a scam.

The same goes for the telephone calls at odd times during the day from people (telemarketers) and companies you don't know. Never buy anything or give any information to someone at your front door or on the telephone that you did not instigate, initiate, or order.

There are logistics to achieve success and peace of mind; a correlation between training and desire. You need a personal drive for education: there is no free lunch. You personally need to find a direction you feel comfortable with and go for it. Above all, do not try to make your personal hobby your profession as this will spell disaster. To begin with, hobbies are things you play at and professions take copious efforts and work.

There are a few statistics that need to be mentioned here. According to the OECD (Organization for Economic Co-operation and Development), our 15-year-olds rank 17th in world science, 25th in math, and 12th in college graduation in developed countries. The United States is 79th in elementary school enrollment and 23rd in today's world infrastructure. As a nation, we are 27th in life expectancy, 18th in having/ developing diabetes, but No. 1 in obesity. A few decades ago we ranked high in all of the important ratings. We are still No. 1 in having the most guns, the most crime, and, by far, the most debt. We have become sclerotic - unresponsively rigid. Wouldn't you think we could be resolute enough at this point to turn all of these statistics around? They have been decades in the making.

People need to reassess their normal life activities, to protect their bodies and their inner organs as well as their outer body functions all through life so their bodies will be able to sustain them well into later life. That said, we generally need to respect our bodies both in the Formative and Productive Years, because who knows how long we will live. For example, if in your teen life you ride motorcycles recklessly for whatever reason and cause injuries to your body; those injuries undoubtedly will cause great pain in later life. The same conclusion holds true for bad diet or drug addiction. You personally have to take control of your life early on. You cannot expect others to do this for you. It is your life and you have to live it responsibly. It is so easy to waste it – waste it because of a whim, a stupid bet, or whatever. Be aware that "macho" is just another word for stupid; it is not the same thing as bravery.

Here is a story from a janitor that ought to wake a few people up.

A young student was put out in the hall for being bad.

The janitor came by and asked "What are you doing out here? Why aren't you in that classroom? What do you see in that classroom?"

The boy didn't have an answer.

The janitor said, "What I see in there are young people learning to be your boss."

That did it. The young man decided that no one in there was going to be his boss. That moment turned his life around.

You are either a part of the problem, or part of the solution: you can't have it both ways. There is no in between – parenting – parenting – parenting – don't blame the teacher.

LYLE'S MEMORIES

When I was ten or eleven, I got the crazy idea to go tear apart an old iron-wheeled tractor that had been parked for a year or so up by the coal sheds near my street. I had an old adjustable wrench (a big one), a pair of pliers, and a couple of other wrenches. I started taking off nuts and bolts wherever they would come loose. It got about lunch time and I wasn't getting very far, but I was determined to get inside this thing. I thought to myself that after lunch I'll go at it again. I had some second thoughts about it while I was home for lunch, so I passed the idea on to my Mom and she said "I wish you wouldn't." That was all she said. Well I was mad at myself for asking and now I couldn't do it. Mom never said no. That was a word she never used. Mom was only five feet tall and she never raised her voice, but she raised five boys alone and did a good job of it. She had more philosophy than money, but it paid off.

Can you imagine a few thousand parents or teenagers reading the above paragraph, turning their backs on it, and not having second thoughts about the ways they are doing things presently?

When I think about growing up in Minnesota, one of the fondest memories I have is the feeling one gets when there is a lazy snow falling, usually in the evening. It isn't really cold out and there isn't a big cold front coming in, it's just a minor local thing that happens early in the winter. You are dressed appropriately for mild winter weather. There is no air movement at all. As you walk along the snow it makes a noise, crunching softly under your feet and you feel like walking for miles. It's not like the twenty below zero snow that is as hard as nails. From my own perspective, I never liked cold weather. I suppose that is because when I was growing up in Minnesota, I had outside jobs (for the most part) and I learned to hate cold weather. This is called accepting the good with the bad – it's part of life.

As the author of this book, I feel my little life is meaningless in comparison with many other lives I have encountered. The depth and weight of some people's gravity is so awesome, it makes you feel good inside – that allows some people to rise to great heights.

I read somewhere that life is what we are alive to. Well, that can be quite a statement, but that doesn't mean what we are alive to has good meaning or moral value. What we are alive to should be the basis for a good life – a life of accomplishment, happiness, and grace.

One of the reasons for writing this book was to find out what makes people tick. What causes them to lead the life style they were or are in? The poor, the rich, those with principles, those without principles, does society play too large a role in people's lives? How does someone with a good upbringing have life collapse on them somewhere along the line? This is why I wanted to get stories from people from all walks of life. Are we just not independent enough, or have we lost the ability to think for ourselves? Some people reach the bottom and pull themselves up out of hole(s) they are in. What affects a person's ideology the most? I feel that if I got the right stories from people, they would help other people immensely.

I have partially read through several books that have similar subject matter to the tunnel of life. The difference basically is that they seem to take a specific subject and go into detail (which is good), but I cover all the subjects that need to be exploited by the young, but not the details. Specifics are for each individual to explore on their own, according to their own composition or what they are inspired to be. I feel that some of what I read would probably go right over the heads of too many teenagers that really need guidance. This book could be coupled with any number of other book approaches, but I have specifically kept my book simple and to the point with the fewest words.

This story is from a guy who thought he had done a bit of good for mankind because he had installed and serviced air conditioning equipment all his life, bringing comfort to thousands of people. But he told me yesterday,

I had a new lens put in my eye. Just think – the eye surgeon gave me my eyesight back. It doesn't get any better than that. Think of the many people that eye surgeon will give eyesight to in her lifetime. What satisfaction she must experience.

If you want to give something back to society, create something of yourself. People that accomplish good deeds have a better feeling about life and, generally, these people live longer lives. As a teenager, why would you not pursue something of value if you have the ability? Why would you not be willing to put forth at least a little effort to make something of yourself, instead of always being *on the take* or looking *for the easy way out*. Drugs, alcohol, thievery, and violence are not solutions, but I'm sure many people will find numerous excuses to protect laziness. Think about it. You are too valuable to waste. But what goes around comes around; and you will have to face it sometime.

FROM SARAH TO LYLE

Ever since I can remember, one of the most common questions asked of me has been "What do you want to do when you grow up?" Now I am a junior in high school and it has hit me that I actually have to start thinking about it. Of course, I have no clue what career I want to have or what college I want to attend.

Although I do, like most others, have a childhood dream that I wish to fulfill. For me, that dream is to be a writer. I'm used to writing fictional short stories, so writing this article is kind of different for me.

If I ever have any free time, I usually can be found writing or attempting to sketch a character from one of my stories (art is not my forte, so it never looks quite right).

No matter what I'm writing, the thing that is most important to me is the development of my characters. I believe that what makes a story unique is its characters, but it is a different kind of character that makes a person unique.

Character can be defined as the attributes that make up a person's nature. For example, some of my characteristics would be that I'm imaginative, organized, loyal, and understanding, but I'm also impatient, incredibly timid, over-critical, and, at times, a tad stubborn.

Recently in school we learned about the characteristics of a leader. Leaders are charismatic and confident. I don't quite have all of the characteristics of a leader and leaders are what the world wants. My parents tell me I need to be more confident; my teachers put a huge emphasis on how important leadership is in today's society. In fact, the slogan of my school is "RAISING THE NEXT GENERATION OF CHRISTIAN LEADERS". I have a feeling that finding a suitable career for someone like me might be harder than I had imagined.

I know that this book is about life lessons and stories to tell that we can learn from, but I'm only 16 and I haven't "lived" a whole lot. I haven't done anything terribly wrong that would make a great life lesson. I am actually the kind of person who needs to be the reader in this situation. I'm the one who needs to have advice given to her so she can follow it.

I guess that's why we are taught to listen to our elders, because they sure know a lot more about life than someone like me does. At times, they can be the leader for us so we don't have to be. I mean, in order for the world to have leaders, there has to be followers like me as well, and I guess that's where I fit in.

Chapter Three

The Productive Years

Your best friend – who is that? Well, if you have your head screwed on right, this should be your answer – YOUR SPOUSE – if you have one. Marriage either works or it doesn't. Marriage is the foundation of life and if it is going to have any future at all, it must be founded in a personal Christian belief. You must be whole yourself before you can live life serenely; before you can have an honorable marriage; or before you can have life with real meaning. If you don't have someone to love, you don't have much of anything. Many people have tried to function by themselves, but not money, work, or anything else will take the place of a mate.

One of the problems you may run into in your Productive Years is that the training you have received may guide you into a job with a future, but in many cases, what is missing is experience. That is what the world is looking for. You may have the knowledge, but how to apply it is something you may not get in college. The transition here can be very perplexing. However, life goes on and the present becomes a very small spot in the past. Your first years in this phase of life may seem groundless, meaningless, and grueling, but those years indirectly teach patience and perseverance. You learn to shoulder set-backs. With time, things just settle down on their own and then it finally happens; you have just gotten your life under way when you meet that very special person who will eventually help to direct and control the rest of your life. Your spouse. Soon children come into the picture, work gets more expanded, and life gets more complicated. The tunnel of life seems to close in on you and decisions are harder to make. But life goes on. Soon there is more joy in life, watching the children grow. Life settles down to a normal pace. There is an intermission here: family life, work, and life's special happenings seem to co-exist. The family takes a trip of special interest, and other things happen of a similar nature. You finally have coordinated all of life's happenings so you can enjoy the full meaning of life. This is the time in life when you create the most memories with the greatest value. The Productive Years are the very fabric of your life. All of the past experiences band together to make accomplishment and success even more possible.

The Productive Years have the most expansion in the qualitative and quantitative values of life. You create more friends and share more activities. Your family activities become deeply coordinated and meaningful. Your children are growing up. Eventually you will say goodbye to them – one by one as they go off to make a life of their own. These are the years near the end of your productive time in life when you take hold of life itself. You reminisce with great pleasure in all the good times and events that have taken place in your life up to now. You take satisfaction in the effort you put into life to make its net worth so valuable. This gives you peace of mind. The tunnel of life only goes one way, there is no turning back. There is no turning back. If you have any regrets, they are yours to live with, but if you build any moral fiber into your life, it will be sufficient.

One day, when I was in Intensive Care (after my heart attack), a nurse came in to check on me.

I said, "My God, you're spoiling me."

She said, "No, my five year old is spoiled. She is my first and I don't know what I am doing. My God, what have I done?"

I laughed and said, "Your desperation is funny, but true reality."

There is no road map for new parents. Sometimes they have to wing it and hope for the best.

This is the area of the Productive Years, where I have put the stories from people that I hope will inspire young people. Some young people may appreciate only one story while other young people will find other stories to their liking and consideration.

FROM J.C. TO LYLE

It is my pleasure to share a story about myself and what inspired me to make my career choices. My dad wants it for this book. The book he's wanted to write ever since his heart attack.

He listens to what people say and follows their actions, and when he finds a heavy, as he calls it, he asks them about their lives, tells them he's writing a book, and asks for their personal story.

He's a lot like my Grandma DeVine in that way. She was a writer too. She made sure a lot of the family history was recorded, even if it was on a scrap of loose paper in her Bible, letters, or a small journal; dates and events were important to her and she did her best in recording her history, at a difficult time during the Depression and afterwards.

My story is much different. When mom and dad moved to California in 1956, I was 3 years old; Loren was 2, and Brian and Aaron were in the future. I was lucky that my parents chose to have been in the right state at the right time. Public schools in Southern California offered the best of education. As children growing up in California during the early 1960s, we had closed circuit TV broadcasts in our elementary schools, with science, Spanish, and Orange County history lessons. We had band and orchestra classes available to us during and after school.

Junior high school brought exposure to a variety of courses, more languages, sewing, cooking, wood working and metal shops; even our own library on campus. It was in 9th grade when we were given a bus tour to a new community college (which had just opened), that caused me to think more seriously about what I was going to do with my future, and if college would be part of it.

High school gave me so many wonderful teachers and such a variety of class choices – music, music composition, history, psychology, government, English, history, and, best of all, independent study. Once again, our campus had its own library, not a convenience at all schools today. By the time I was preparing to graduate, our local community college had representatives traveling to the high schools to promote college programs that led to various careers. One of the programs that interested me was their stewardess/hostess. After two years you received an Associate of Arts Degree and interviews with a variety of airlines, domestic and international. It was hard work, but I got my degree and was hired by United Airlines in 1973.

Throughout the years of my education I worked weekends, holidays, and summer-time. I left home at age 21 and looked forward to starting my new life secure with a good education, employed by a solid company, and the future in from of me.

If I could offer a suggestion to the next generation, it would be to make the most of your opportunities. This country has much to offer. Take the time to get involved. Giving back is something my family has always supported – it makes sense and you feel good about helping others.

My suggestion to the state of education is to offer more vocational courses. This is good for business, and for young people just starting out in the world.

It takes commitment to one's goals and honest hard work to make a success of yourself. If you are willing to accept that responsibility, you will be happy and most successful.

FROM BRIAN TO SON KEVIN

The longer I experience life, the more respect I have for that little word "Attitude" and how greatly it impacts one's life. It's more important than how we look, what we know, our successes and our failures. It is more important than what people think of us and it can make or break a business, a church, or a home. We cannot change the past, but attitude will guide us and help to dictate our future. We can learn something from every event that takes place in our lives. We cannot change the way others think and act, for that is their choice. The one thing we must choose is whether we approach the events in our lives (whether they may be good or bad) with a positive or negative attitude. You see, WE

ARE IN CHARGE OF OUR OWN ATTITUDE!!! I am convinced that life is 10% of what happens to us and 90% of how we react to situations. I am very proud of you; more proud than any father could be of his son. I am convinced that you will go far in life for you have that potential. As I have said to you many times as a young man, "Always know right from wrong before making a decision." Go through life having fun, for fun is part of one's success in life. In closing, I share a quote from Grandpa Lyle, "If you have your morals straight, a good work ethic, and a positive attitude, you will be successful."   ---Love, your father, Brian

FROM JOHN F. IMSDAHL
CIRCLE OF LIFE

I was born the last of three children to parents who were at the age where they were more interested in retiring than in playing with me or showing me how things were done. My mother was completely engrossed in her religion and my father was more interested in being with his friends than doing things with me. Growing up I was never told that I was smart, or good-looking, or that I had to try to make things work for myself. If things did not come easy, then I assumed I could not do them at all. And, because I lacked the love and devotion of my parents, I was not capable of standing up to the cruelties of other classmates' rebukes or criticisms. So I always thought I was not as smart, or was too ugly or just not equal to others my age.

Money was never given to me; I always had to earn it. It began with a small allowance for mowing the lawn, and when that was not enough, I sold fruit, had carnivals in the back yard, and later, I had paper routes from my earliest age until I was well into high school. While in high school I worked at the local car wash on weekends and at Gerber Baby Food Co. during the week. I would work at anything to earn money.

One day (I was thirteen and delivering papers) I ran into Harry Del Rosso's Christmas Tree lot with a "Help Wanted" sign. I had often asked Harry for a job, but he always said I was too young to work for him. But I persisted and he finally gave me a job. I did everything Harry asked me to do. I set up trees that had been knocked down by the wind, replaced Christmas lights, and whatever else he needed. I sold a lot of Christmas trees for him. One day I showed up for work and Harry got right in front of me and started yelling that I stole $50 from him. I must have looked like I was innocent, because Harry calmed down right away. Later, I remembered that his friend Dave had trouble breaking a $50 bill the night before, and when I told Harry, he knew it was Dave that had stolen the money and he never did come back to work. Harry always trusted me after that and one day he asked me if there was any way we could sell the biggest tree in the lot. I said sure. Harry owned several airplanes at the Hayward Airport and he offered an airplane ride to anyone who sold that big tree in the lot. Well, two hours later, I sold that tree and won the airplane ride. Harry took me to his airplane mechanic's business where he owned at least 6 planes. He picked out the largest one and told me to get into the left seat. He showed me how the rudder worked, magneto, and radio settings, and he had me taxi the place to take off. We took off with me partially at the controls and we did a landing pattern and he guided me through the landing. Within 3 months I would taxi and fly all of his planes, taxi them into the service bay, and I was selling parts and services behind the counter of the mechanic's business. At any one time, I would have keys to over 30 airplanes that I washed and made ready for doctors, lawyers, and accountants to take their planes up for a weekend trip. I made very good money doing this job. At 13 years, I could not receive a licence, but I got a student's permit the day I turned 16 – the same day I got my driver's licence and bought my first car, a 1951 Ford. I had a Honda motorcycle that I could drive from the age of 15·1/2 to deliver papers at 5 am, and a '51 Ford to run errands for Harry. I was making money. Harry Del Rosso was patient and enjoyed teaching me how to do things. Harry became my adopted dad. I enjoyed being around him because I felt I was not dumb, or ugly, or incapable. With Harry, I had purpose and could do things.

I was a poor student at San Lorenzo High School and I wish now that I had not wasted my time there. I had wonderful and caring teachers that saw great things in me and potential that for some reason I did not want to act upon. If I had it to do over, I would study harder for better grades, play more sports, learn other languages, play more music and act in more plays. But for some reason high school did not grab my interest. I spent too much time at the airport, and/or delivering newspapers to take an interest in high school.

What I was interested in was flying airplanes, so when the Army suggested I join to become a Warrant Officer helicopter pilot, I enlisted. I joined the Army because the Draft Board was getting close to "drafting" me. Things went well and I enjoyed the officer candidate life and flying helicopters. But I caught a cold, which went into pneumonia, and I went into the hospital for five days. I should have accepted the fact that I missed so much flight school that I could not continue with my flight class, but I tried to work overtime to make up for what I had missed. This didn't work and I was not allowed to continue. This crushed me because I was sent off to the Infantry school and so missed the opportunity to come back and join Harry in his business. When I came home from Vietnam in July 1970, having survived a year with one of the most decorated recon infantry units in Vietnam, I did not have the 2000 flight hours from Flight School. So I never went back to visit harry because I had lost my opportunity to fly *and work with him. I was ashamed – my one chance to make my life worthwhile and fulfilled was taken from me. I also came home to friends who did not go to Vietnam, but were hooked on drugs and living dead-end lives. I did not want to be around them, so I only stayed a week with my parents.*

I packed my bags and moved to Monterey, California. I had been introduced to Monterey as a result of a scuba diving class I had taken there, and I loved the area. When I got to Monterey, I immediately applied for a job at the Hyatt Hotel. I started at the bottom as a busboy, then room service waiter, and finally got the best job – bellhop. I met movie stars, sport stars, top musicians, race car drivers, professional golfers, and all the rich and famous of that time. I studied how they ate, how they talked and how they acted in public. I studied everything about the rich and famous because I wanted to be rich someday too. I applied to Monterey Peninsula College in my first week there. I was accepted, but was placed on probation because of my poor efforts in high school. I was on probation for only the first semester because I got all As and Bs. I loved MPC and my professors. I soaked everything up and did so well that I graduated from the University of California at Berkeley with a Bachelor Degree in Business and a minor in Political Science.

The University taught me a lot about business and finance, and although I wanted to go to law school, I chose to take a break from school after I received my Bachelor's Degree. As a senior, I participated in 36 on-campus job interviews with stockbrokers, bankers, retail companies, and insurance companies. One interview was with three young guys who had made fortunes in San Francisco real estate. They were not that much older than me, but were having the time of their lives. The whole idea was attractive to me so I decided to have a second interview at their office in San Francisco.

The Tunnel of Life

I began my real estate career in March, 1976, and never went back to college for my law degree. Investment real estate was fun and rewarding. I enjoyed San Francisco and my real estate career led me to sell small apartment buildings, large condominium complexes, and even five hotels. I worked in San Francisco and Hawai'i, selling millions of dollars in real estate. But markets change, and I failed to see the crash of 1980 coming. Even after owning two homes in San Francisco, a condo on Maui and another on the big island of Hawai'i, I was going broke fast because I was not making the income to support my "little empire". I was working in real estate during the Great Real Estate Depression from the early to middle 1980s, but still going broke. The Prime Interest Rate had gone to 22% and no-one was buying real estate. As I looked around to see what I could do next, I saw that my real estate appraiser friends were making money. "Hard Money" was being lent at high interest rates, and in spite of the market, banks were lending at 17.75% to homeowners. To become an appraiser I had to take more classes, but I still had to make a living, so I took on work as a hotel employee, and sold TVs and Stereos in a store for 9 hours a day.

By 1982, I was beginning to become an appraiser, and by 1986, a bank hired me as one. I worked for the bank five years to get to know how to be a good appraiser while understanding what loan underwriters did and thought of appraisers. The experience was very valuable, and by 1991, I was ready to start my own appraisal business. Owning your own business means long hours (18-20 hours per day, sometimes 7 days per week for weeks on end), but the financial rewards allow Judy (my wife) and I to travel the world mainly in first class. I live on a gentleman's farm as I have always wanted to do, and I am financially independent. Working hard while you are young allows you to not have to work at all as you become older. As 2011 neared and past,

I began retirement. I look back on the last 20 years as saving my financial life and helping me to live the life I always wanted. In the end, I worked almost 50 years of my life. I was never automatically successful in my life; I had to learn many things the hard way; things did not fall into my lap; however, I do believe persistence is the key to success. You must find your way by trying hard each and every day. Somehow, someday, even when all else seems to fail, you will achieve your goals by determination and persistence.

So, when you are down and out, when things look the bleakest, you really do have to pick yourself up, dust yourself off, and go at it another way. If you do that often enough success will find you. But you will never find success by lying in bed or on a couch, or feeling sorry for yourself, or by trying to take other peoples' money. Success only comes by being persistent.

DECEMBER 31, 2010 – KATRINA

This is a story about a young man, Troy Powell, who escaped the horror of Hurricane Katrina by only a few hours. Even so, he still had to go through quite a lot. I think this story has its own credence, even though he didn't suffer like most people did in Katrina. It shows how people will band together in time of peril. Their true underpinnings and basic moral fiber shows. It also reveals how people find a special love for a particular area – most people cannot be moved with a bulldozer from where they live, because they are so rooted in the land.

On the second anniversary of Hurricane Katrina I wanted to write my story. I lived in the upper Ninth Ward/Bywater area of New Orleans. I had worked late on the night of August 27th and went to bed around 1:00 AM. Katrina, at that time, was a Category 1. I was awakened by my good friend Terry Conerly, who

29

called me to say that the storm was now a Category 5 and that he was evacuating and I was to go with him to his mother's house in McComb, Mississippi. Terry knew that I did not have a car at the time and he was not going to allow me and my dogs stay in the city. This was a whole day before Mayor Ray Nagin issued the mandatory evacuation for the city. Terry gave me just one hour to get my things together, so I packed the usual evacuation bag – three days' worth of clothing, my hurricane box with personal papers like credit card statements, income tax filings for the past three years, insurance papers, some food and toys for the dogs. It took us 18 hours to get to his mothers' house. Normally, it would take only an hour and a half. There we waited for the storm.

Monday morning when Katrina came ashore we went outside to see what was going on. We could hardly stand up in the wind. The trees were bent almost sideways. Then the 'eye' came over and it was eerily silent. What I remember almost immediately after the storm was the smell of pine, heavy in the air. We had no power at Ms. Verla's house, but we did have running water. Terry's sister Gwen had power, but no water, so we would all take showers at Ms. Verla's in the morning and stay at Ms. Gwen's during the day in the a/c. Terry and I stayed at night at his mother's house, gathered around the battery radio listening to find out what was happening. We got most of our reports from my parents in Hawaii when they could get through on the phone. Remember, there was no power or cable TV to watch. One day, Terry and I went to the First Baptist Church to get ice that was being handed out by Marines. We were in line with about two hundred other people, waiting for ice. After we got our allotment and were walking back to the house, Terry turned to me and said, 'What a humbling experience that was, waiting for a bag of ice and four apples.' I will never forget that moment as long as I live

– that overwhelming uncertainty of what the hell is going to happen to us.

After the second week, I got a call from my brother Brent. He wanted to know how far Jackson, Mississippi was from where I was. He told me I needed to get to the Flying J Truck Stop on Interstate 20 in Jackson by 5:00 PM to meet a truck from his company and that Warner was going to get me to Phoenix. I said OK and Terry's family scraped up enough gas to get me there, and to get Terry back to McComb. I will never be able to repay Terry's family for their kindnesses and help. It was truly hard to leave them, but as they pointed out to me, this was a time to be with family and that I was welcome there anytime.

I met the first of seven drivers that day. It took two days to make the trip to Phoenix. I had to change drivers every 8 hours. They were so nice to me and my dogs – checking to see if we had to pull over for them to walk (or relieve themselves) or if we were hungry, to stop and get something to eat. The truckers would not let me pay for anything. Just writing this brings tears to my eyes. As I said before, it was a very humbling experience. It renewed my faith in humanity. We got to Phoenix just in time for the birth of Brent's son Justin. It was God's way of having me there in my family's life for that momentous time. I stayed with Brent and Jeanene for about three weeks and found an apartment of my own. Mom and Day helped me go back to New Orleans to retrieve my things after we found out that I could go back into my area. My area did not flood, so I was very lucky. We packed up my things in their motorhome and headed back to Phoenix. The government did not help me much because I was a renter, so my family came through with money and support. I had taken a class in balloon designing the year prior to Katrina and my instructor contacted me to see if I made it out alive. Ms. Linda Kiss was instrumental in getting me on my feet. She sprang into action and contacted many of her former students and a "flood" (pun intended) of donations came streaming in: everything from small donations of money to balloon equipment and food, and treats for my dogs. (They were in Scooby Snacks for a year.) I found a job with Pacific Events, a production company like the one I worked for in New Orleans, but the city was calling to me like a siren of the sea, singing her melodic song to come home; so in September of 2006, I moved back to New Orleans.

My old job and friends were waiting for me. We got to the city on September 25, 2006 just in time for the kickoff of the first Saints football game in the renovated Super Dome. The city was electrified. We could feel the hope in the air. I think it put my mother a little at ease to see the city so alive. My parents were apprehensive about me moving back but still supported my decision.

I told people in Phoenix that "I'm a Northerner by birth, but a Southerner by choice." I was very easy to identify by my Southern accent (acquired in the 12 plus years I lived in the South), so Phoenix community didn't know what them. There are things you take for granted in the region in which you live – like asking for a buggy (that's a shopping cart), butting in on someone's conversation in the grocery line, or calling everyone Mr. so and so, or Ms. Whoever, and, heaven forbid, calling a woman Ma'am. That one threw them for a loop. "Don't call me ma'am," I would get all the time. The folks in Phoenix are not used to someone who respects their elders or, as a matter of fact, has good manners. All in all, I am very happy to be back in the city I truly love to be in. With all the negative press, it is still one of the best places in which to be and it will take (God forbid!) another storm to make me leave the Jewel of the South. I truly know what it means to miss New Orleans.

* * *

This is a story from a man that in my opinion has the most logical approach to life there is or can be.

AARON'S CHALLENGE TO THE "EVERYTHING IS BLACK OR WHITE" ARGUMENT.
EVERYTHING IS GREY!!!

While a minority of people would probably state that they agree whole-heartedly with the idea that every decision, action, or problem falls into a black or white scenario, it seems this is a quite common outcome. Political and religious leaders, business leaders as well as the rest of us state their opinions and thus their personal actions and decision on a yes/no, good/bad, black/white basis. Many times it is done to simplify complex issues. This may be a good starting point, but one quickly sees that complex issues call for complex solutions; which, by definition, are not black or white. They are almost always some shade of grey. After a college logic class, political science class, and several business psychology classes, as well as a few years of business experience, I have come to see problems and solutions as being on a sliding scale versus a choice of "A, B, or C". Examples abound in politics. Is abortion choice or murder? Should medical care be private for some or public for all? What is important to most of us is decision making for our personal lives. For example, one can prepare to work as a business finance manager. If that job is unavailable, you may work at a company doing collection. You decide to try to become an accounting manager, but due to changes in the company, downsizing (rightsizing) and new business lines, you don't have that opportunity. You may have to switch to another business function to try to move up there. It happens again. The solution: A good worker will always have a place in the company. Don't try to plan your whole career as it will not happen as you plan it. Don't live without any plans day to day as you will never get anywhere. Be flexible and live in the grey area to have consistent work and build a reputation as you go. You will probably enjoy work more as you won't be bored by the same job decade after decade.

Most would agree that success in one's career is a worthwhile goal. However, what the exact meaning of success and failure are can be tricky to define. In a general sense, a career or job is a requirement for most people in order to survive in the world today. It is simply a way to earn sufficient pay for shelter, food, clothing and other assorted costs. It is all too easy to see success as an amount of money earned or position obtained. But this simple approach does not take into account that life is not just about work and sleep. A healthy personal life with free-time, personal relationships with friends and family, time for hobbies and spirituality should also be considered necessary as a sign of success in anyone's life. A balanced life seems to support the claim we should not attempt to attain traditional success or failure (black or white), but we should fall somewhere on the sliding scale with a balanced life (grey). This is not to say that enjoying one's work is wrong. But if life were all about work, why would there be weekends and holidays, or, for that matter, why would one retire? Given that, most of us know the well-to-do relative who never has time to take a vacation or travel for holidays. He may have money but most people would not consider his life successful. Similarly, there is usually someone we know who does little to secure their future, works inconsistently, and never worries about anything. They seem to always enjoy life fully. This is probably not the success most of us are looking to obtain either. It's pretty easy to see that a mix of these two relatives would suit most of us. The challenge for us all is to find our spot on the sliding scale of wants, needs, and priorities for our own successful lives.

* * *

This is a story about a young pharmacist whose younger years probably should not happen to anyone. The only salvation for her was her mother's ability to control and smooth out each negative incident as it happened. This story shows how Christine rose above adversity and became a greatly productive and positive person.

CHRISTINE'S "FLYING TURKEY"

I had just won a turkey dinner complete with all the sides. I was a shy sixth grader in Brooklyn, NY. My school thought it would be a good idea to give away a complete turkey dinner. To win this turkey dinner, you had to guess the full cost or price.

Mr. Horowitz, our gym teacher, who was also standing in as the announcer at the assembly, had just called my name out loud. A few seconds before he uttered my name, I announced my own name under my breath so that only the person next to me heard it. You should have seen the shock on my face when Mr. Horowitz spoke. I thought I heard fireworks outside in the school yard – I was so happy. Being that it was November, it was more like the sound of wild turkeys than popping fireworks.

Everyone clapped for me as I walked to the front of the stage. I had never won anything in my decade-long life before. Mr. Horowitz said I guessed the price to the penny. I couldn't wait to go home and tell my mom (after all, she was the one who would be cooking it).

Mom's reaction was predictable when I got home that afternoon before Thanksgiving break began. She hugged me and told me how happy she was for me.

When Thanksgiving morning came, she woke up early (before the sun) and started to prepare this unlucky bird. First she gave it a bath, throwing it into the sink, scrubbing it really well (as she did her children in their baths – minus the bubbles, of course). Then she put it into the oven to roast.

Finally lunch time came and in our house that is when we had our turkey dinner.

Mom carefully placed the browned and juicy turkey on our rectangular-shaped oak coffee table and set it up as best she could. We lived in a small apartment in Brooklyn and there was no room for a dining room or table.

Dad, a slender average-sized man, was sitting on the couch beside the coffee table and, as usual, he was wearing his angry face. He was in the position I knew only too well – holding his knees with the palms of his hands. Being 10 years old and the eldest child of four, I knew what was coming next.

Mom noticed his face, but as the soldier she was, she put on a smile for her children. Just as we were about to sit down to eat, Dad grabbed the edge of the coffee table and in one easy swop he flipped the table, and the turkey went flying, stuffing and all. Yes, it was flying across the room in slow motion in my memory. Before then, I didn't know turkeys could fly, but Dad, a hardworking Lebanese immigrant, showed me turkeys can fly.

Mom, as usual, did not say a word about the scene before her. The upside-down coffee table, the broken glass, and the twice unlucky turkey now lay splattered on the floor. I already knew the routine: Mom would usher my 8 year old brother, 6 year old and 3 year old sisters into our room while she went back to argue with Dad. It was more like Dad yelling and Mom crying.

QUN'S STORY

This is a story about a Chinese girl named Qun. Her family lived in the province of Yunnan in China. When Qun was two years old, China was in great turmoil (1966 – 1976). Families were separated, and people could be shot for no apparent reason. Qun's mother and father were taken away, probably because her mother was a doctor. Her two older sisters were sent out to the country to work in the fields as were many others. Many were abused, some married, and some never came back. The men were never encouraged to seek professions, such as carpenters, electricians, etc.

Because Qun was only two years old, she was left to be cared for by her grandparents. Children at that time did not get much schooling. China put out a book written by Chairman Mao called the Red Book, which promoted very controlled thought. In her early work years Qun worked for a tobacco company. Yunnan Province has an ideal climate for tobacco growing and many young people worked in this industry. Qun eventually got an education (including college) in China, taught school for a while, and also worked as an interpreter with the tobacco industry. This was because most of the tobacco processing equipment was from England and the workers had to be trained on how to use it. During the time Qun got her education, English was the prime language taught, but prior to that time, the language was Russian.

Qun was married for a short time in China and had a son. Later she met an American and married again in China. It took 2 years for her to get clearance to come to America in 2003. Qun taught Chinese in Garden Grove, CA grade school for 1·1/2 years, and then worked for a Chinese company that was doing business between China and the U.S. Later, she worked for Costco while going to Saddleback College, and while a student, worked in the College cafeteria as a cashier. After completing her schooling as a phlebotomist, she was employed as such by Saddle-back Hospital, where she also does laboratory computer processing. Her son is 19 years old now and going to college. He plans to be an electrical engineer.

So you see, life can have its problems along the way, but some people just rise above them and reach success as did Qun.

FROM MAC TO LYLE

Introductory Letter – *The first day of school is always exciting but this one started to unravel quickly. The announcements had just ended and the students were asked to stand for the Pledge of Allegiance.*

One student refused to stand. I was shocked. Patriotism is one of my most treasured values and as soon as the Pledge concluded, I questioned his actions. He didn't recite the Pledge because he felt it was wrong to promise to be loyal to a flag. I requested that he at least stand in respect of the flag. Again he refused. The class could feel my astonishment. I spoke again to the student before he left Homeroom, but it was obvious there would be no compromise.

The following day, after morning announcement were over, I read "The Children's Story" by James Caldwell to my class. It is a powerful story about a classroom of students who give up all their freedoms because they never fully understood the meaning of the words in the Pledge and the fragility of freedom. I took the time to teach the meaning of every word in "The Pledge of Allegiance". We discussed patriotism, and the flag and its symbolic representation of our nation's beliefs and promises. On the third morning when the PA system announced the Pledge, my entire class, Jordan included, rose and placed their hands over their hearts and respectfully recited the Pledge to their Flag. It was a powerful moment because they now all understood and embraced the hope our Flag represented.

It's Monday afternoon and it's been a long day. I'm tired. I stand outside my room greeting my last group of glassy-eyed students, when Jorge suddenly flies by me, smiles, takes his seat and exclaims, "I love this class! I've been looking forward to it all day. What are we going to do today, Mrs. Devine?" I am reborn!

Those perfect days are the ones that keep you going. They begin with everyone present, well-rested, with all their supplies in hand. All my technology works perfectly and all of theirs is left at home. I begin with a quote connecting it to a compelling story that ties in beautifully with the poem I've chosen. They are inspired to respond in writing and you can taste the flavor of success – it is so palatable. The lesson flows as I connect the objective of the day with an article from the daily newspaper. Discussion ensues as they hone in their verbal and reasoning skills. Everyone is actively engaged as I circulate and interact individually with each and every student. Students work collaboratively before they fine-tune their joint efforts into individual responses. As the lesson concludes, they write down their homework assignments with confidence because they already know how to do it. "That's going to be easy!" I hear someone whisper, not realizing that we just spent the last hour making it EASY. Those are perfect days. They don't happen very often, but just the thought of one is enough for me. It is what I envision every day for my students for I am the consummate optimist. Some days we even achieve it!

When students enter my room they sense the energy and excitement. It begins with someone being chosen as the "Student of the Day". A red toy is placed on their desk with a hand-written note by me praising them for a past accomplishment or encouraging them to be successful today. This note is always shared with the student's friends and they smile in appreciation of the compliment.

I am a gifted storyteller and I use this gift to pull my students into my world as I expand theirs. I see opportunity in every piece of media. Comics are perfect in teaching figurative language: newspapers contain relevant human-interest stories that provide students practice recognizing elements of a story. I strive daily to widen their interests, push their limits, all while grounding them in their own community. I readily recognize that at least one grain of potential exists in each of them and my goal is to focus so much attention on that singular gift, they too begin to see it in themselves and own it for a lifetime.

Brenda was a student in my language arts class and she taught me an important aspect of education. Brenda lived with her illiterate grandmother and fifteen relatives in a two-bedroom house. She worked every afternoon cleaning houses with her grandmother and in the evening, she was given multiple tasks to complete at home. She aspired to be a psychologist and was driven to learn; however, whenever she tried to sit and read, the room was either too noisy or she would be accused of "faking" it. I tried to intervene on her behalf by assigning detentions after school so she could complete her reading logs. It worked at first, but eventually her grandmother began to question all the detentions. It became clear that Brenda was going to have to find a way to solve her problem. I felt helpless.

Surprisingly, Brenda returned after Winter break with all of her missing reading logs completed. She told me she had found a quiet, hidden place to read in her neighbor's pool. She wasn't floating on a raft, but rather sat on the bottom of the deep end of a drained pool, with a book light, reading. I learned an important lesson. So succeed, students must be active, and accountable. As much as I wanted to help Brenda, the most I could do was share the possibility of a dream and offer support. In the end, Brenda accepted the responsibility and created her own success.

Professional Biography – *Each year I have my eighth grade students write themselves a letter stating their goals and ambitions for their future. They write about their fears and accomplishments, their failures and successes. I write my own note to each student, without their knowledge, and slip it into their envelope. I store these letters away for four years. Every May, these letters are mailed to graduating students of the Santa Ana Unified School District, reminding them of whom they were and who they planned to become. Each year, students return to see me and discuss their letter. Sometimes there are tales of regret; but, most often, students regale me with stories of their high school successes and triumphs.*

I do this, because as a child, I attended parochial schools and I remember thinking, "there's got to be a better way to teach". I wanted to become a teacher because I knew I could make a difference and I knew I could inspire kids to learn. My passion for learning and my creative nature were well-suited for a career in education. My first teaching position was in a private school where I had the freedom to teach the way I believed students needed in order for them to learn. I loved to immerse my students in their learning. On Columbus Day, I dressed as Columbus, outlined the Niña, the Pinta, and the Santa Maria on the floor and assigned students to the "ships". They stayed on the floor all day eating hard tack, learning about navigation, reading Columbus' biography, calculating math on an abacus, and creating a binnacle. By the afternoon, they had learned about scurvy, mutiny, tyrants and social injustice.

Believing in my own mantra that I could make a difference, I left my private school to teach in Santa Ana. I was ill-prepared for the many hardships my students face, but I was more deter-

mined than ever to bring creative lessons and meaningful relationships into their lives. Making that personal connection with children is one of the keys in their success.

My first teaching assignment in Santa Ana was a self-contained sixth grade class of newcomers. I didn't speak Spanish and they didn't speak English but, together, we worked through our language barriers and created the inside of an Egyptian pyramid in the classroom. First, we designed a maze by covering the desks with murals the students saw in books. They learned how those colors were created as they practiced drawing Egyptian art. Every student chose an Egyptian identity and wrote about their life. We studied hieroglyphics and Egyptian numbers. We provided tours to the rest of the school and proudly wore costumes and hand-made Egyptian-style jewelry. At the very center of our tomb was King Tut, in all his finery.

I teach the standards as I unlock the creativity and imagination within each student, something that is often overlooked by today's society. I listen and learn about the Hispanic culture while I share my Irish heritage. They are shocked to learn that my family immigrated to America just like theirs. I explain that America is filled with immigrants from all over the world; the only difference is the years we arrive.

Each year, I make it a point to discuss the Irish belief in leprechauns. I watch their eyes widen with awe as I share stories of the "wee-people" and the mischief they create on St. Patrick's Day. By the time the seventeenth of March arrives, they are primed to believe the unbelievable. This particular year I secretly placed a drop of green food coloring on the inside cap of my water bottle. I asked one of my sixth grade students to hand it to me and as he did the water turned green! Eyes popped, mouths opened, and creativity and imagination were reborn. This was contagious because the following day one of my students reported that a leprechaun must have followed him home because after he relayed the story to his mother, his own milk turned green that very night. Imagine! That is my gift to the teaching profession. I could never just teach: I create, inspire, encourage, and impact my students with poignant stories that pierce their hearts with belief in themselves.

Upon returning from a recent trip to Hawai'i, I brought back shells that I found on the beach, one for each of my students. I told them it was the beginning of their collection of world treasures and that they must continue to build this collection throughout their lives. I reminded them that the key to this collection is their education and that that key can unlock any door. These students will be reminded of this important fact when they receive their May letters in two short years. I am confident that by then they will have learned what I have learned...that dreams do come true and that you can always make a difference if you work hard enough and believe strong enough. Together, we build a community of learners that is supportive of the individual and the collective successes each has achieved.

Student Progress – I have a student in my Strategic English Language Arts class this year that has made significant gains in her education. Upon entering my eighth grade class, "Karla" was performing at the Basic level as measured by her California Standards Test scores for the past three years. Although she had consistently tested at this level, I knew that she had more potential. After the first month of school, Karla was still working at the Basic level as evidenced by her first benchmark score. I knew at this point that I had to differentiate my instruction in order to provide Karla the support she needed to achieve proficiency.

A quiet student, Karla is reluctant to respond aloud. My first goal was to get her talking. I paired her with another student *who was working at the Proficient level. The A-B pairing strategy is designed to encourage students to talk. After targeting Karla for several weeks with this strategy, she began to participate more in class and she was demonstrating a new level of confidence. When I "cold-called" on her, she was more willing to respond. By discussing her thoughts with her partner and using a sentence frame written on the board, Karla is now able to present her thoughts in an organized way. These oral responses have allowed Karla to formalize a concept for her writing and reading activities.*

Karla's CST scores showed a weakness in the areas of word analysis and literary response. Her writing lacked organization and did not include transitions, topic sentences, or a thesis statement. To address these deficits, I focused on writing a lesson objective containing academic vocabulary, which Karla would copy. Thinking maps were integrated into the lesson and color-coding strategies were used to emphasize the appropriate structure of a written response. Daily lessons were assessed through the use of "exit slips".

At first, Karla was usually held after class for reinforcement of the lesson's objective. She is now able to demonstrate her understanding of the objective without additional support. Recently, Karla scored a huge victory when she scored Proficient on the District Writing Assessment!

Through this case study, my teaching has improved. Analyzing the data of my students helps me to understand how to better meet their needs. Focusing on specific students' performance has led to an overall increase in my classes' performance as measured by the most recent benchmark exam. I am confident that there will be similar growth demonstrated on the upcoming California Standards Test and I am excited to see how well my students perform.

"Daniel" was an obese, immature student who had been diagnosed with an auditory processing deficit. He was mainstreamed into my language arts and social studies classes mid-October. This English Language learner scored early advanced on the CELDT test and, even though he was reading at the tenth grade level, his writing skills were at the fourth grade level. As an eighth grader he faced two major challenges. He had to pass the District's U.S. Constitution Test, and score 'proficient' on the District Writing Proficiency Test.

I started with his writing skills. I used Thinking Maps to help him organize his thoughts. The Maps enable students to "see" and, therefore, to organize their thoughts in a meaningful way. This type of scaffolding worked very well with Daniel's visual strengths. Once he understood the framework and the basic steps, we practiced sentence structure. By the end of the eighth grade Daniel scored an impressive 7.3 on the WCJ III Form C. He passed the District Writing Assessment as Proficient.

To pass the U.S. Constitution Test, we used index cards. The key terms and definitions were placed on the front of the card and illustrations on the back. These manipulatives gave him the hands-on experience while providing a visual representation of the information. Thinking Maps were used to show the cause and effect relationship between important historical events. With these tools, Daniel was able to pass the U.S. Constitution Test on his first attempt.

These classroom successes carried over into Daniel's personal life. That spring, he came out for the track team that I was coaching. He was still obese, but that didn't stop him. He showed up to practice daily and completed all the drills. He had the slowest time for the mile run, but he won the admiration of his team. When a child starts to build a history of success, it becomes a way of life. Daniel never performed well enough in track to compete in the city track meet, but on the last day, when he was running the mile, the entire team stopped stretching just to cheer him on. At the end of the season he lost ten pounds, gained friends, and created an improved self-esteem. These victories were more important than any medal or ribbon he could ever have won.

School-Community Involvement – *Most of my students have never traveled more than five miles from where they have grown up. Their view of their community, and their world, is grossly underdeveloped. I want my students to have the opportunity to experience the world around them; not just their immediate environment. I read the newspaper daily to them so they can begin to develop an awareness of their community. We follow the stories day-to-day, week-to-week. Recently, we followed the story of Maddie James, a five-year-old Dana Point child diagnosed with inoperable brain cancer. My classes were especially drawn to her story and everyone was truly crushed when we read that she had died. The news said Maddie's parents were trying to raise 1.3 million dollars for the Dan Point Marine Institute, a favorite place of Maddie's. My class had been recycling to earn money for an end-of-the-year party, but upon hearing of Maddie's death, the class unanimously agreed to donate our entire savings of $84.26 to Maddie's cause. Most of my students have never been to the Marine Institute but each of them gave from their hearts. Incredibly, the word spread and fellow students at McFadden brought us their empty water bottles. Through this loss, my students' sense of community and their world has grown.*

This sense of community service has been developed by a number of opportunities that have come my way. These include:

- *Serving in the "Step-up Program" for three years at McFadden Intermediate School. Each year I mentored students who were at risk and involved them in cross-age tutoring with students from our neighboring elementary school.*

- *My sixth grade class at McFadden raised $300 for the "Make A Wish Foundation". Although this may not seem like a lot of money, each penny was a sacrifice made by my students with the hope that it would make another child's life a little easier.*

- *Belonging to the "Corazon" church group and traveling to Mexico to donate food, presents and Christmas gifts to the poor.*

As with Maddie, each of these activities has been motivated with the sincere belief that even the smallest of acts, when well-intentioned, can make the world a much better place.

Philosophy of Teaching – *William Butler Yeats said it best when he wrote, "Education is not the filling of a pail, but the lighting of a fire." Teaching is the means by which that fire is started. Providing the direction and support, which allows students to connect in a meaningful way to the world around them, keeps that fire burning. It was during my summer vacation that I actually realized my philosophy of teaching. I was earning money during the summer selling "thank you" gift boxes to car dealerships. One aspect of the sales world is something called power lunches. Sales People gather over lunch to network. As they went around the table introducing themselves and discussing their jobs and positions I just couldn't bring myself to say I'm JUST a teacher. I told the assembled group that I was a "sales manager". My company produced "educational products" and I had one hundred twenty "employees" working directly un-*

der my supervision. I met daily with each person and personally oversaw every piece of work they produced, and prepared weekly progress reports. In less than a year's time, I was so successful that all my subordinates were promoted to the next level with a 98% success rate. Needless to say, the lunch table was impressed. Until that point in my life I had always thought of myself as JUST a teacher.

The rewards of teaching are unlike any other profession. Compensation is paid in the success of our students, not in cash. One of my past students reminded me of just such a success. The children in my third grade class in private school were under a great deal of pressure. Their parents were making financial sacrifices on their behalf and they expected results. Unfortunately, the result was a class fearful of failure. I created the "Golden Treasure Chest Card". Akin to the Monopoly game cards, this one could get you out of trouble. I gave one to every student and told them that if they should receive an "F" or get in trouble, that card had the power to save them. I would use all the power I possessed to remove the low grade or resolve the problem. Of course some students needed to use their cards the same day they were given them, but the rest put them in a safe place until needed. Ten years later my husband and I were purchasing tickets at a local movie theatre when the young man behind the window asked, "Mrs. Devine?" I nodded and he said, "Look!" With that, he pulled out his wallet and showed me his Golden Treasure Chest Card. He told me he just couldn't bear the thought of throwing it away. These are the special rewards of teaching, touching a child's heart in such a way that they are set on fire for the rest of their lives.

Education Issues and Trends – *I believe one major issue in public education today is accountability. We must have accountability with our schools, our teachers, our parents, and our* students. While there is a lot of focus on schools and teachers, what about the students? They, too, must be held accountable for their education. Students fail because they are allowed to fail. They are not held accountable. They have seen so many F's that FAILURE has lost its impact and they have lost their ambition. Society spends a great deal of time and money focusing on school and teacher accountability and rightly so. It does, however, forget to focus on the students; and, because of this, many students opt out of their responsibility to learn.

To address this flaw in our educational system, I propose we eliminate grade levels and develop a system composed of "Levels of Learning". With the advent of state and national standards, it would be relatively easy to impose such guidelines. Once a student has proven success at one level he proceeds to the next. There is no failure per say, students study until they are successful. Their education revolves around their learning and they are held accountable for this learning. When students realize they must learn or they simply will not move on in school, they become accountable.

Students who aren't held accountable aren't engaged in learning. They adopt an apathetic demeanor and become passive to the process. Regardless of their failure, they are moved on into the next grade level or course with no reliable predictor for future success in place. By incorporating a clear set of assessments for student learning we can turn this around and put the child on the pathway to success.

In the real world, there are real consequences for failure. The motto of the Sana Ana Unified School District is "Failure is not an Option, Success is the Standard! It is up to us all!" This motto is brought to life every day in my classroom when students have to retake tests to earn a passing grade, have to complete certain tasks to be dismissed from class, and have to stay after *school for tutoring when their grade falls below a "C". They are learning more than how to conjugate a verb or the results of the Civil Way. They are leaning to take responsibility for their education; they are learning to be accountable for their learning.*

The Teaching Profession – *People comment how "wonderful" it must be to be a teacher. After all, you work short hours; have several vacations a year, and your summers off. All I can say is "They are partially right, it is a 'wonderful' profession, but not for their reasons." I'm not sure why society in general tends to label teachers according to our vacation schedule as opposed to our accomplishments. Teachers have an enviable calling. We work with the hopes and dreams of the future. We find that hidden talent or morsel of interest and build a rainbow out of it. We don't work – we inspire, create, dream, envision, and guide. It's amazingly rewarding to directly see the results as we help students' metamorphosis and ignite their passion to learn.*

A teacher's day begins hours before the students arrive and lasts well after they are gone. We aren't presented with a willing student body every day, but rather we're competing with a fast-paced, technologically- advanced world that needs us more than ever to ground children in the real world and engage them in their own education. This is especially true in high school and middle school as we work with over-stimulated, sleep-deprived individuals that would define the classroom as some sort of sensory deprivation torture. The title Teacher isn't quite as simplistic as it sounds. Teachers do more than just explain ideas. When asked, "Who was your favorite teacher?" we can quickly reply with our favorite teacher's name, grade level, and how they touched our lives. Those special teachers don't stick in our minds for the knowledge they instilled, but the connections they made. They did more than explain a concept; they put themselves in our world and touched the soul of our self-worth.

The Productive Years

Teachers possess super powers of passion, integrity, and optimism. We are counselors, social workers, nurses, judges, life coaches, magicians, nutritionists, and motivational speakers. When students from the past spot us, they immediately ask, "Do you remember me?" The real statement is I remember you! You touched my life. Several years ago I was surprised to receive a letter via school from a student I taught in third grade. She was nervous because tomorrow would be her first day teaching in her own third grade class. Maria wanted me to know that she want to be just like me as a teacher and she thanked me for the inspiration to become a teacher. Being a teacher is no easy task, but it is by far the most important job our society has to offer because we shape the future with our instruction and develop role models for future citizens.

It is unfortunate that there are just a few ways for teacher accountability to be assessed. We live in a world that wants to see the proof, the data, and the numbers, which measure our effectiveness. Much of our accountability is based on the annual California Standards Test. However, there are no measures for all the other roles we play in our students' lives. That doesn't mean we aren't accountable; in fact, we are probably more accountable than any other profession…the average thirteen-year-old student is most unforgiving. We have a tremendous responsibility to be accountable. We are accountable for the standards we teach and the safety of students while in our care. We serve as role models for behavior, attitude, and professionalism. My father commented once, "Don't worry that children aren't listening, worry they're always watching." I've taken that advice to heart and constantly self-monitor my behaviors to reflect the values I believe are most important to instill in our youth.

One of the most exciting parts of the job is to be a student yourself. Although I have been teaching for over 30 years, I re-

cently went back to school to obtain my Masters in Curriculum Development. It was exciting to have the opportunity to work with fellow "teacher-students" as we honed our computer skills and learned the latest trend in education. It's challenging to keep abreast of the best practices and rewarding to create a lesson using the latest technology.

Much of the teaching profession relies on collaboration. In college, I learned "what to teach". Through collaboration, I learn how to teach. Last year I was selected to be a Thinking Maps trainer for my school site. This training as enabled me to be a mentor and a resource to my colleagues. As a trainer, I author and present workshops while offering support on a one-on-one basis.

I'm also a department chair for 8th Grade Language Arts. As such I host meetings where my team and I design and collaborate on upcoming lessons. We work collectively, sharing ideas and offering one another support. As a member of the Instructional Leadership Team my responsibilities include mentoring fellow teachers and acting as liaison between the Principal and the staff. In my role as an ILT member, I have presented several workshops with information I've learned from reading the book, Teach Like a Champion. *I find it challenging and motivating to present new ideas or simply review those we've forgotten. Good teachers not only motivate students but also each other. I model for my students and my teachers that most hallowed of all goals, to be a life-long learner.*

Teaching isn't a job or a professions; it's a calling. It's a calling to reach out to a child and make a difference in their life. We're there to right a wrong, embrace a dream, support the challenged, encourage the dismal, and spark the fire of learning in all our charges. It's all covered under that one word, "Teacher" and I'm proud to stand in that number.

National Teacher of the Year – *America is a nation of individuals who share the same belief that all are created equal and endowed by our creator with unalienable rights...life, liberty, and the pursuit of happiness. Our schools must reflect these values if we are to continue to be a nation unsurpassed in the free world. Our classrooms cannot afford to be swayed by the political world but must remain steadfast to the Founding Fathers' vision of America. Quite frankly, I'm tired of hearing that our schools and education system are lagging behind other nations. We are the only country in the world that insists on educating 100% of its population all the way through high school. During that time teachers instill the beliefs of individualism and creativity. In the name of test scores we are strangling our students by the noose of accountability, destroying the very programs which develop creativity that is no necessary in today's world.*

We must continue to believe in the ingenuity of the American way of life by aiding our youth to find their individual strengths as they become a contributing citizen. By constantly comparing our great nation to others, we are sacrificing the very ideals that make us unique and enviable. As teachers we are and always have been accountable to our students and we are equally accountable to one another as we push to excel. But we aren't the only stakeholders in the formula. There are parents, administration, and communities. We all have a shared obligation to the future generation. Our students will continue to be successful because they are learning to embrace the American way of life, and our schools and educators see those successes every day.

In the words of Felix E. Schelling, "True education makes for inequality; the inequality of individualism, the inequality of success, the glorious inequality of talent, genius; for inequality, not mediocrity, individual superiority, not standardization, is the measure of progress in the world."

Our school system is an extension of our societies' beliefs. We believe in an equal opportunity for every citizen but every citizen is accountable for their own success.

We're teaching standards as well as a belief system, which made this country great. Benjamin Franklin recognized the importance of education as he inspired our country's first settlers to become enlightened. He ignited the American spirit to become who and what you want.

We don't have cookie-cutter classrooms that press out dozens daily; we provide a portal of potential. Teachers today have futuristic vision and an undying belief in the American way of life. I am proud to be an American and even more proud to be the gatekeeper for future Americans.

FROM CHARLES TONER TO LYLE

I received a call recently from an old friend from my boyhood named Lyle Devine. That telephone conversation generated a flashback in time – the 1930s, 70+ years ago. It was the era of the Great Depression. Lyle and I lived in the same neighborhood in the small farming community of Slayton, Minnesota. Slayton is located in the extreme southwestern corner of the state. Our house was adjacent to U.S. Highway 59 that found a route through Slayton. This highway traversed the western side of Minnesota from the Canadian border to the Gulf of Mexico.

Lyle lived just two blocks away on Mill Street. Mill Street was the first street north of the tracks and perpendicular to U.S. Hwy. 59. It acquired its name from an old mill which sat at the far end of the street and overlooked an old dried up lake bed that, in its day, was called Lake Elsie. The mill was now abandoned and had seen better days.

In that flashback, I recalled how we and at least a dozen other kids would while away the summer seasons during the height of the Great Depression. It was indeed a dark period in American history with so many willing to work but no work to be found. As youngsters between the ages of 8-12, we didn't experience the last 1930s like the older teenagers and adults. But, we did live it and in our own way. You can bet that most kids went barefoot in the summer and when school started you were back into shoes. Our shoes were either hand-me-downs or, if you were most fortunate, a new pair from the local mercantile store.

These were the kid years, 1938-1941. Then in December, 1941, our country became fully engaged in WWII. As brand new teenagers, we quickly lost our adolescence and became adults overnight. In short order, there were very few men around town. They were either drafted into the military or moved on into a defense job until the draft caught up with them. As a consequence, the teenage boys (even the 13-year-olds) were expected to step into adult roles to fill the job market. Lyle and I chummed as kids and seemed to jump into various jobs together. The first job, as I recall, was weeding a neighbor's garden. The wage earned was around 15 cents each. We then moved on to working as basement rats at the local mercantile store on Saturdays. Generally, there were four of us and our job was to carry stock from the basement, haul groceries to the farmer's car, candle eggs, and at the end of the day (typically 10-11 PM) sweep the floor. Pay for a day's work was $2.00. Actually, it was $1.98 as they took out two cents for Social Security. Mr. Jit Lowe was the store manager and he looked to our well-being and kept us straight although I'm sure we caused him some grey hairs. Case in point: When we got hungry, we would set a can of soup on some hot coals in the furnace to warm it. On several occasions, we would forget about the soup can and it would explode, shaking all the gravity-fed piping throughout the store. Usually, by the time the dust settled, Mr. Lowe was in the basement inquiring as to what happened. We *were busy candling eggs and didn't have a clue – hadn't heard a thing.*

Early in the summer of 1943, Lyle and I teamed up with Paul Skully and we traveled 130 miles south to Algona, Iowa to detassel corn for the Pioneer Seed Company. The pay was 50 cents per hour. Our supervisors were kids just a couple of years older than us, perhaps seniors in high school. The Company gave us a cot, a blanket, and put us up in the local school gymnasium. We were in hog heaven as there were hot showers available. Our stay lasted just two weeks, so we hitch-hiked back to Slayton. We then landed jobs with the local Log Cabin service station, and soon leaned the intricacies of vulcanization, fixing flats, changing engine oil, and pumping gas. Mr. Clarence Taarud was the owner/manager and taught us skills we never thought we were capable of doing. Pay had now increased to $30.00 per week in the summer, or $12.00 per week during the school year. The work was rough and dirty, especially when a farmer came to town with his tractor-mounted corn-picker, trailing four or five corn wagons, and wanting some tires repaired or changed on a cold muddy November day. This job lasted one winter and two summers.

The following year I received a call from Mr. John Christiansen, owner of the local creamery. Soon, I was the local milkman, up at 4 AM to deliver half the town before school started. During the summer months I learned the rudiments of churning and printing butter, making a cream route through the county twice a week, and muscling 400 pound blocks of ice out of the ice house twice a week. As I recall, during this time frame, my old boyhood chum, Lyle, was now operating the film projectors in the local movie theater, and another old chum, Dale Roteman, was firing up the ovens in the local bakery and starting the first batch of bread each morning.

The Productive Years

In 1945, WWII finally ended with Germany surrendering in May and Japan in August. Although the veterans were coming home in big numbers, there were still plenty of jobs during the summer months. And so it went for the next few years. Lyle graduated a year ahead of me (1946) and shortly thereafter, enlisted in the Army. That summer (1946) found four of us assembling eight 90-foot towers for the baseball field. Once they were assembled and raised into place by a crane, we made the climb to install the reflectors and bulbs. As I recall, there were 96 bulbs and reflectors that needed to be hoisted to the platforms and installed, some 90 feet up. Our pay was a rousing $1.00 per hour.

My first year out of school was in retail trade in a small, local grocery store (Assistant Manager), followed by 18 months learning the wet-wall plastering trade before moving on to the County Engineering office and being introduced to the art of surveying and drafting for road and bridge construction. It appeared to be the perfect job. You were indoors during the winter months drafting and estimating cuts and fills in road construction. The spring/summer/fall season generated plenty of outdoor activities on preliminary and topographic surveys, setting slop stakes and finishing up with blue-top surveys for the road contractors. As an apprentice, I leaned the intricacies of survey instruments, locating benchmarks, running the 'chain', and drafting.

By mid-year 1950, my life and those of seven school chums changed rather rapidly. The Korean War ignited in late June and we, a 'gang of eight', enlisted in the U.S. Air Force, departing in August 1950 for a new venture in our young lives. We had grown up as group; but our departure in August signaled the last time we were together as a group. An era ended and a new one began – for the rest of our lives.

To this point, what I have attempted to convey is a picture of life in a small farming community, with thoughts that life as a youngster was mellow, but guided by many forces. And to this day, I feel most fortunate to have grown to adulthood in a small farming community (as compared to living in a larger urban setting). In this very small metropolis, everyone knew everyone, and everyone knew everyone's business – both public and private. That has to be considered the trade-off when living in a small community – there were no strangers.

With that in mind, I hope to convey how these older citizens affected me and my buddies' day-to-day activities. They touched every young person during their Formative Years. At the time, being young, naïve, and frisky, I never realized the impact the town fathers and mothers played in molding my life and future.

There are numerous names with many and varied personalities that come to mind when I think of the small town where I grew to adulthood. Several names were mentioned in the preceding paragraphs and, in one way or another, they each had an effect on my life and being. But, I must add to those names the many in the town that provided direction and substance, and helped to mold character into the skulls of the young adults in the community.

Above all, the parents did the guiding and set the stage. The rest of the community did a great job in putting the frosting on the cake. Some names that come to mind, who were masterful as helping to frost the cake, were:

Miss Velz *– School teacher (social studies, history, and mathematics). If you goofed up, her favorite weapon was either a 3-sided or heavy broadsided ruler across the knuckles. Your choice. She had a heart of gold and would teach anyone the art of crocheting (even the boys).*

Ed Beckstrand *and* **Lawrence Ness** *– School teachers (music).*

Ted Rothwell *– School teacher (mathematics)*

'Buzz" Earlandson – *School teacher (wood-shop & high school sports)*

Joe Budde – *Businessman (operated pool hall and supervised paper routes)*

Tut & Mary McDonald – *Business couple (the Silver Star Grill – favorite hangout for eats and dancing during the war years and beyond)*

Tracy & Pep Hafner – *Business couple (Drug store & soda fountain, sports)*

Bill Schfranski – *Businessman (Bowling alley & lunch counter)*

Copie Hagen – *Retail sales at various businesses in the community*

Dr. Pierson & Nurse Dorthy Krumm - *Medicine*

Ada Smestad – *Retail Sales*

Steve Stephenson – *Businessman* (Dill Elevator Co.)

Les Nelson – *Businessman (Furniture & Mortuary)*

'Pop' Terry – *Rural mail carrier and sports enthusiast (Golden Gloves boxing & high school football)*

Jim Davey Lowe – *Businessman & neighbor (Hatchery)*

Harry Peters – *Businessman (Men's clothing)*

Andy Hardiman – *Auto dealer (Olds, Cadillac)*

Paul Ruans – *Retail Sales*

'Dude' March – *Assistant County Engineer*

But I must say the true cake artists in our development were our mothers – **Anna Toner** *and* **Sadie Devine**. *These hardworking, patient, and loving women worked tirelessly, day after day - cooking, cleaning, baking, gardening – doing their best to keep their families fed and together during very hard times and poor living conditions. From them, we learned what hard work really means and that there is always enough food for another* *hungry moth, even if that mouth is that of a stranger... Yes, those two ladies were the true masters on frosting the cake.*

This story of the past was so well-written I wouldn't think of disagreeing with a word of it, but I must admit, for the most part, I've tried to keep this book about other peoples' lives. However, this story showed how we grew up developing multiple talents as young people, maybe far ahead of our age, but everything changes with time. What was important in that time has gone by the way of the wheel, and the hammer and chisel. Today the young are in tune to electronics, new marvels and challenges.

My boyhood friend's name is Charles Toner. He rose to the rank of SMSGT in the Air Force and later received a technical degree in college. He continued to work with the Air Force as a civilian. The U.S. Military Service offers many opportunities for the young if they are inclined to a service life. I know several people that had their successful lives molded by starting in military service.

A Sergeant Major is the next to the highest non-commissioned officer in the army; a Command Sergeant Major is the top (I believe the army has only one or two of them). A Sergeant Major is one of the most revered, honored and respected foot soldiers in the army. He is responsible for the smooth running of the army, and you might say he is the "baby sitter" for the army. He understands all the proper procedures, functions, and codes of the army and what makes it 'work'. Officers may tell the army **what** to do, **where** to do it and **when** to do it, but it is the Sergeant Major who tells them **how** to get it done.

* * *

I met Timothy Goodman when we served on jury duty. Some people just stand out. In addition to this, Tim helped me when I misjudged a curb and fell, which caused my shoulder to become dislocated. Tim called an ambulance and notified the Court of my mishap. Later he and Rob (a retired policeman also on jury duty) would walk me to my car each day to be sure I didn't get into any trouble on the way. They are both very accomplished individuals but don't make note of that, because it isn't part of that little phrase of life - THE POWER OF WE AND ME. Here is Tim's story.

THE POWER OF "WE" AND "ME"
BY TIMOTHY GOODMAN

My earliest recollection of struggling through my speech impediment was when I attended Yorba Linda Middle School. More specifically, in Mr. Lee's math class and Mrs. Yerian's English class. My impediment was a type of stalling; being stuck on the first word and not even being able to stutter it out. It was humiliating. It often looked like I couldn't speak or read. I couldn't present anything orally in class, call my friend's house and say "Is Heather there?", read scriptures out loud in Sunday School, or start up a conversation with someone I didn't know and sometimes even with someone I did know.

Later, as a recent graduate from high school, I was faced with a choice that would pit me against this devastating struggle and later alter the course of my life: would I transition directly into college or serve a proselytizing mission for my church? As a missionary I would leave behind "purse and script" to teach people about the word of God and the doctrines of the church to which I belonged. I would likely be called to serve far from home. My

contact to family and friends would be limited to mail corre-
spondence and two phone calls a year. I would serve for two
years and work full-time for six days a week from 9:30 am to
9:30 pm with one day set aside for shopping, cleaning, writing
letters, etc. During that time I would be talking to strangers,
knocking on doors, doing oral presentations, speaking in church,
teaching lessons, calling people on the telephone, and working
with local church members. In addition to amplifying my prob-
lem with communication and public speaking this type of mis-
sion also seemed contrary to all the advice that most high school
graduates receive when they face their post-graduate future.
Usually, speeches at high school graduations are filled with
words like "the world is YOUR *oyster,* YOU *are in the driver's*
seat now, discover YOUR *passion, or follow* YOUR *dreams." While*
I do respect this time of a young person's life as important self-
discovery, I also believe this time is fertile ground to cultivate an
unhealthy 'what's in it for me' mentality. Daringly, I decided to
face my fear, leave all things behind, and serve a mission.

My mission assignment called me to serve in the Colorado
Denver North Mission. The first quarter of my mission was
probably the most difficult. My speech impediment didn't mirac-
ulously disappear as I hoped it would. Instead it seemed worse as
it was coupled with unrelenting rejection and loneliness. As time
went on, my mission president extended assignments to me that
pushed me to my limits. I was asked to serve in a variety of lead-
ership positions including Assistant to the President and Mis-
sionary Trainer. These assignments were very challenging be-
cause they required me to train and model effective communica-
tion and presentation skills to both veteran and newly called
missionaries. Additionally, I was expected to fulfill leadership
responsibilities on top of my already busy load of being an every-
day missionary. I accepted all of these assignments and never

once used my speech impediment as an excuse or reason to say no. Little did I know, this choice would change my life forever. Eventually, I had so much work to do and purposes to fulfill that I didn't have time to wallow in my fear or inabilities.

By the end of my mission, most missionaries and people I interacted with had no clue that I was once a victim to a debilitating speech impediment. In fact, on the contrary, I was often complimented on my ability to make conversation, teach missionary lessons, train new missionaries, and present at conferences. However, nothing could hide my physical exhaustion. My knuckles were red, my suits were torn, my shoes were worn to the bone, I lost about 15 pounds off my already slender build, and I could fall asleep anywhere at any time. Miraculously, to this day, my fear of speaking and my speech impediment are near to gone. Every once in a while it will rear its ugly head, but only when I need to be reminded of the lesson learned on the streets of Colorado.

Lesson learned: become anxiously engaged in something bigger than yourself. When you do, you'll find that your unrelenting insecurities and fears become dormant and your hidden talents and abilities take full sway in not only you, but in the world around you. For me it started with my mission, later my profession and still later with my family.

Popular columnist and author David Brooks suggests that the purpose of like is not to find yourself, but to lose it. He later warns that too much expressive individualism like building your resume or being more concerned with "me instead of we" often leads and distracts people on their journey towards success.

As I've done my best to remain anxiously engaged in causes that take me outside of myself, my journey has taken me to places I would've never seen from the beginning. Currently, I teach third grade and absolutely love it. In both my career and person-

al lives I serve in leadership roles that allow me endless opportunities to lose myself and serve others.

In my downtime, I've also been known to travel the country speaking to young people and adults about self-esteem and individual worth.

You, the reader, may not believe me. I understand. I may not have believed it or paid much attention to it myself. The phrase itself is an oxymoron: lose yourself to find yourself? But from someone who walked the walk and paid a heavy price, I challenge you to do the same. You may not have the same reasoning or the same outcome, but you will learn that by focusing your efforts on the power of "we", you'll discover the true power of "me".

* * *

The following is an autobiography of a very gracious farm-girl writer whom I have known all my life. I have followed her story with three very heart-warming editorials from the public domain.

FROM ELEANOR WARREN BERGLAND TO LYLE

I was born into a farming family of three children in Minnesota; not a large farm by any means, but we lived comfortably. My father suffered two strokes which required us to move off the farm into a small town of about fifteen hundred people. We went from having a comfortable existence to a more reserved existence. My father survived the strokes but was an invalid for seventeen years. My mother took care of him (no rest homes then) and put the three of us children through high school. I had high hopes of attending a beautician school but never got there (we couldn't afford it).

I married and had three children of my own. Life has been good to me.

The Productive Years

I lost my husband after forty-one and a half years of marriage. After his death, I had my house moved into Slayton. Four years later, I remarried and moved back onto another farm and another good life.

I have been a farm wife for about sixty years. Farming used to be fun and a farm was a good place to be, but I hear fellow farm people say that farming isn't fun anymore. It costs so much to stay in the business. Most wives are working off the farm to help make ends meet. Some wives on the farm are like hired men – milking cows, driving tractors, hauling grain to town, operating combines, besides doing all the household chores and transporting the children miles to all their activities (scouts, ball games, float building, music lessons, church activities, swimming lessons, doctor appointments, etc.

One day, Mr. Orville Klasse, president of the Murray County Historical Society of Slayton, Minnesota called and asked me if I would be interested in helping in the museum. I said no. I really didn't have the time. I had a family of three and I was helping to take care of my mother-in-law.

Mr. Klasse didn't give up and kept calling me. I finally said yes. After several weeks, I became interested in county history – I was hooked! It was about the same time that I started scrapbooking and I have now donated about 200 history scrap books to the museum.

I eventually was employed by Slayton's weekly newspaper, writing a personal column for a time; then I went into compiling a column of county history. I enjoyed it very much and the people who read the paper loved it.

Now I am eighty-seven years old and make my home in an Assisted Living place. I truly wish that I were able to continue compiling history.

My two employers were Seth Schmidt and Gerald Johnson.

The Tunnel of Life

From the writings of Eleanor Warren Bergland for the Murray County newspaper.

This is a little something that most people in my home town would be interested in, but it is evident of how the entire United States was involved in our biggest war, WWII. Even little Slayton, Minnesota, a town of just over 2000 population, had a defense plant.

Mayor E.J. Gustafson, who was also Governor Stassen's state representative at the Chicago Ordinance plant, called Slayton in August 1942 to let them know Slayton was to have a defense plant. The city owned lots near the farm sales pavilion, so that particular site was chosen for the plant.

The first unit of the plant was 35 x 125 feet. Since need of the building was immediate, the structure was made of wood and concrete floor. From the time the ground was leveled to the actual operation of the first piece of machinery was 14 days. The Slayton Farmer's Lumber Company and the Botsford Lumber Company provided the lumber and the labor.

The part to be manufactured was known as an adapter booster and was used in bombs. Out of 250 applicants, about 50 people were employed having some knowledge of how to operate a lathe. The first three women to be employed were Mrs. Claire Hendrickson, Mrs. Curt Loudon, and Miss Thelma Olson. My mom's good friend Anna Toner also worked there.

The plant started operation in late 1942 and the article didn't say when it closed, but it must have been near the end of the war.

In February 1946, it was sold and used as an auto and farm machinery sales store, and a pioneer seed corn store. Later the building was sold again (in 1955) and it was used as a furniture store until 1963 when it became a general farm store (which it still is today). The town of Slayton still has a population of just over 2000 people.

A Message for Youth –
A Message for You, Son, From an Iowa Judge

These are words which anyone's son might never hear until too late. An Iowa attorney presents them as adapted from remarks made by a district judge, while sentencing two high school boys. The youngsters had thoughtlessly made a practice of borrowing autos to go joy-riding. The article is presented here for parents, who may wish to impress their own sons with the importance of obeying the law. These are strong words, but much easier to take second-hand than from a judge, however kindly, speaking man to man from the court bench. Here is the text:

"You come from good homes, both of you. E-, I have known your father for many years and I have for him as much respect as for any man I know. I do not know what attitude he has taken about this at home, but since your arrest he has gone about his work with his face as full of sorrow as if there had been a death in his family.

You retain his love, but you will never again have his full respect and confidence. There will never be a time when you are away from home, when he will not have a feeling of fear, and wonder about what you are doing.

H-, Mr. R- tells me that your family is as good as E-'s. You may be sure that things I say apply equally to you.

Now you have been convicted of a felony. A felony is a crime for which you might be sent to the penitentiary. In this case, I do not have to send you to the penitentiary. The law gives me the choice of sending you to Anamosa for one year, to the county jail for six months at hard labor, or to fine you $300. Because you are only 16, I can send you to Eldora instead of Anamosa.

Because this is your first conviction and because you are not infected with venereal disease, I am permitted to give you a parole. The law does not allow parole for persons infected with venereal disease nor for offenses other than the first. Never again will any court have the right to parole you. But if you never see the inside of the penitentiary or jail, you will not have escaped from the penalties of your crime. You stand convicted of a felony. The record of your conviction will be here as long as the courthouse stands.

No amount of good conduct in the future can ever erase it - next year, or ten years from now, or when you are old men. If you are ever called to be witnesses in any court of law, some lawyer will point his finger at you and ask this question: 'Have you ever been convicted of a felony?' And you will hang your head and admit that you have, because if you should deny it, then the record of these proceedings will be brought up from the vaults and read to the jury. And the questions will be asked of you for the purpose of casting doubt on your testimony. Convicted felons are not believed as readily as other persons.

It may be that someday you will have a chance to get a job in one of the expanding countries of South America, and you will apply for a passport. You will not get it. Canada might allow you to come in for a two-week fishing trip, but you will not be allowed to stay. No country will allow you to become a resident. Your world is Oh! So much smaller than it was. Some day you may seek a position in the civil service your state or of your nation. On the application blank you will find this question: 'Have you ever been convicted of a felony?' If your answer is not truthful, it will be detected, because appointments are made only after investigation. The record is here to be fond by anyone interested.

Someday you may want to take a position of trust, where a surety bond is required. On the application for the bond will appear this question: 'Have you ever been convicted of a felony?' And while you go from one bonding company to another trying to find one willing to take a chance on you, the position will be filled by some applicant who has not been convicted of a felony.

In a few years you will be 21, and others your age will have the right to vote, but you will not. Your father may be a candidate for public office, but you will not be allowed to vote for him. The members of your political party will not be interested in you, because you will have no vote to give. You will be a citizen of your state and your country, but you will have no voice in public affairs. It may be that someday the governor will pardon you and restore your rights, but it's going to be humiliating to ask him. He'll want to know your whole record. It is a bad one.

Your country is calling men to the colors. Its need is such that men are being drafted. But the army will never accept you, nor will the navy. Military men are proud of the service; they will not permit it to be debased by the enlistment of convicted felons. You may serve your country in a labor battalion, but never behind the guns. Yours may be drudgery of way, but never the honor that comes to a soldier.

I am granting you a parole. A parole is in no sense a pardon. You will report to the men who have accepted your parole as often as they may ask, and at such times as they may ask. Your convenience is not a matter of importance; you will answer fully and truthfully any question they may ask. Should they suggest that you refrain from going to certain places or with certain companions, you will follow their suggestions without question and without grumbling.

You will obey your parents. If your parents send you to bed at 9:00 o'clock, you will go without complaint. You will perform such tasks as are assigned to you. Should the slightest complaint of your conduct reach this court, your parole will be revoked immediately and you will begin serving your sentence.

You will not be brought back here for questioning or explanations. You will have no opportunity to speak to this court. You will be picked up and taken to prison without notice to you and without delay."

~ from a Nebraska Newspaper

A CANADIAN SPEAKS UP

Editor's Note: *The following editorial was broadcast recently from Toronto, Canada, by Gordon Sinclair, radio and television commentator. At this time (and at every time) of American travail, this inspirational expression should bring comfort and appreciation.*

This Canadian thinks it is time to speak up for the Americans as the most generous and possibly the least appreciated people on all the earth.

Germany, Japan and, to a lesser extent, Britain and Italy were lifted out of the debris of war by the Americans who poured in billions of dollars and forgave other billions in debt. None of these countries are today paying even the interest on its remaining debts to the United States.

When the French franc was in danger of collapsing in 1956, it was the Americans who propped it up, and their reward was to be insulted and swindled on the streets of Paris. I was there, I saw it.

When distant cities are hit by earthquakes, it is the United States that hurries in to help. This spring, 59 American communities (were) flattened by tornadoes. Nobody helped.

The Marshall Plan and the Truman Policy pumped billions upon billions of dollars into discouraged countries. Now newspapers in those countries are writing about the decadent, war-mongering Americans.

I'd like to see just one of those countries that is gloating over the erosion of the United States dollar build its own airplanes.

Come on, let's hear it! Does any other country in the world have a plane to equal the Boeing Jumbo Jet, the Lockheed TriStar or the Douglas DC10? If so, why don't they fly them? Why do all the international lines except Russia fly American planes?

Why does no other land on earth even consider putting a man or woman on the moon?

You talk about Japanese technocracy, and you get radios. You talk about German technocracy, and you get automobiles. You talk about American technocracy, and you find men on the moon – not once, but several times and safely home again. You talk about scandals, and the Americans put theirs right in the store window for everybody to look at.

Even their draft-dodgers are not pursued and hounded. They are here on our streets, and most of them (unless they are breaking Canadian laws) are getting American dollars from Ma and Pa at home to spend here.

When the railways of France, Germany and India were breaking down through aging, it was the Americans who rebuilt them. When the Pennsylvania Railroad and New York Central went broke, nobody loaned them an old caboose. Both are still broke.

I can name you five thousand times when the Americans raced to the help of other people in trouble. Can you name me even one time when someone else raced to the Americans in trouble? I don't think there was outside help even during the San Francisco earthquake.

Our neighbors have faced it alone. And I'm one Canadian who is damned tired of hearing them kicked around.

They will come out of this thing with their flag high. And when they do, they are entitled to thumb their noses at the lands that are gloating over their present troubles. I hope Canada is not one of them. ~*Gordon Sinclair, December, 1973*

THE CONCERNED AMERICAN

What kind of America will you have? We have had the 'Tired American'. We have had the 'Forgotten American'. We now have 'THE CONCERNED AMERICAN'. He is one of those long-silent people, who have become soul-sickened as to what is happening to their America, knowing for the first time the dank chill of fear as to what the future may hold.

For the first time in his life, THE CONCERNED AMERICAN is having nightmares at noonday, worrying about whether his America can survive.

THE CONCERNED AMERICAN is bitter because the un-loosed holocaust of inflation from reckless government spending has made a shambles of his hard-won savings and his Social Security checks.

THE CONCERNED AMERICAN is fearful that he is being swept along, as by flood-tide, by forces against which he is powerless to resist.

THE CONCERNED AMERICAN is troubled by the belief that his government is only telling him the truth when it suits its convenience.

THE CONCERNED AMERICAN is frightened because his government has become one where political cronyism has replaced blindfolded Justice; where corruption in high places has become more of an accepted way of government than individual enterprise and competition.

THE CONCERNED AMERICAN is fearful that false prophets in government have led him down strange paths of illusion and that, in truth, we are becoming a hapless, floundering, second-rate power...where inability to defend our country or our dollar finds us in helpless confusion.

THE CONCERNED AMERICAN is a frightened American, not frightened for his own physical safety, but that of his children's children and millions of Americans yet unborn. He is angered that the jackals of the human jungle, that prowl our streets with immunity and impunity, have made it impossible for the citizenry to walk American streets without risking assault or death.

THE CONCERNED AMERICAN is a soul troubled at the thought that too often, heroism is something only to be jeered at, that decency has become covered with filth, that honesty and integrity and patriotism are to be held up to the blasphemous ridicule of the unwashed mobs as being only for squares.

THE CONCERNED AMERICAN is on edge in his distrust of glib politicians who openly pander for votes by painting a glittering oratorical mirage of total illusion.

THE CONCERNED AMERICAN is fearful of super-smooth politicians whose policies are as fickle and un-certain as the weather-vane whirling in the changing direction of a vagrant breeze. He remembers that one aspirant to the White House once oratorically boasted that he could "personally lead a mighty good revolt".

THE CONCERNED AMERICAN has a well-humbled Bible as he listens to the candidate say he is not beholden to anyone for the policies he espouses – he remembers that Isaac once said, "The voice is Jacob's voice but the hands are the hands of Esau."

The voice may be that of the candidate, but the hands are the hands of Lyndon B. Johnson. And THE CONCERNED AMERICAN wonders if Americans haven't been duped into trading, like Esau of Biblical times, their precious birthright for a mess of political pottage.

THE CONCERNED AMERICAN is concerned about too many of his countrymen that seem to have a childish faith that there is a God-given guarantee that America will always be a great democracy that will exist in perpetuity. They forget that eternal vigilance is the price we must pay for liberty and that 16 great civilization have crumbled into the dust of time...not from assault but from decay from within.

THE CONCERNED AMERICAN yearns for a leader that will restore decency and integrity to government, a leader that will save America, rather than squander her strengths, a leader that can be a 20th century Moses in leading his people to a new and greater future.

THE CONCERNED AMERICAN knows it will take stout-hearted leaders, because we are now paying the price for listening too long to the siren song of the demagogues that promised the easy, painless way out of the problems facing America.

THE CONCERNED AMERICAN knows that America stands at the fork in the road of destiny, that the hour is five minutes till midnight and that the decision can no longer be put off as to the road we must take.

THE CONCERNED AMERICAN knows the terrible loneliness of frustration as he says, "What can one man do?" He should know there are tens of millions with the same agonizing concern for America's future and safety.

THE CONCERNED AMERICAN should know too, that he and his fellow patriots have an all-powerful weapon – greater in its might than any army…a little piece of paper…an "insurance policy" to safeguard America's future – A BALLOT.

THE CONCERNED AMERICAN can wield that piece of paper and end his noonday nightmares because he holds the mighty weapon that can restore America to the paths of righteousness, decency, and un-bounded glory for all humanity – HIS VOTE. The battleground will be the hundreds of thousands of polling places from border to border and coast to coast.

THE CONCERNED AMERICAN can turn this country around from its headlong plunge to disaster, and save it from the fumbling clutches of those so bankrupt in political principles that they would do anything and say anything to win an election.

THE CONCERNED AMERICAN can put this nation once again on high secure ground where honor, justice, patriotism, decency, equality, truth, courage, integrity, and devotion to God and country are words of pride and once again meaningful.

THE CONCERNED AMERICAN sees in Richard M. Nixon a man of honor, integrity, ability and courage that can turn this United States of America around and restore it to the greatness every American prays for with all his heart. Richard M. Nixon is the leader that spells new courage and hope for THE CONCERNED AMERICAN.

~*Guest Editorial by Alan C. McIntosh, author of "A Tired American Gets Angry". Star-Herald, Luverne, MN (10-24-1968)*

Note: *Currently, the meat of this editorial is probably three times as true as it was when it was written. The only thing that didn't turn out was that the Nixon administration was just as bad as the other party.*

INTERVIEW WITH BILL DOCHNAHL

This newspaper interview is more of a partial biography of this man's life. It deals with his early life experiences, education, and life endeavors: (although I suppose the Vietnam War may have changed his life endeavors because this interview goes into his retirement years). Now, if you want to appreciate retirement as this man does (even with cancer), you have to live a worthwhile life, and a good retirement is just an extension of a good life style. Bill Dochnahl's love of music and his dedication to family provides special human interest. (I've known Bill most of his life and I never knew he had a Purple Heart medal and a few other commendations. It took me years to fully realize what a great guy Bill is.)

Question:BILL, WHERE DID YOU GO TO SCHOOL?

Bill: *La Salle High School (a college prep private school in Pasadena, CA), Pasadena City College (AS degree, Architectural Design/Drafting), California State University Los Angeles (BS degree, Public Administration/Urban Planning), and University of Southern California (graduate program, Public Administration/Urban Planning).*

Question:WHAT DO YOU DO?

Bill: *I'm retired – and lovin' it. I work to keep from easily slipping into idle time that's effortlessly tempting. To stay off the couch, my energy is driven by innate creative-centered passions placed on hold during my long (yet satisfying) career. The new journey: (a) OSU Extension Master Gardener's Program and volunteer; (b) freelance landscape design; (c) writing a monthly gardening article for the Umatilla County Employees' Newsletter; (d) working on a short story trilogy; and (e) editing my Vietnam memoirs. And, of course, I'm my dog Pogo's ball thrower.*

Question: WHAT IS THE BEST THING ABOUT YOUR WORK?

Bill: *Any of the work I do now in retirement is all designed to revolve around my core passion and need to be creative in some productive way; with time now to contribute to my community, reaching out and feeling someone has been touched in some positive way.*

Question: WHO IS THE LIVING PERSON YOU MOST ADMIRE?

Bill: *At the risk of getting detained in front of St. Peter's Pearly Gates, it is Jesus. After visiting with Jesus for a while and trying to get the date and time of the Rapture (just to be prepared before 'the blink of my eye'), I then would time-travel forward to* *when Mark Twain wrote his Mississippi River Classic novels to be an understudy to this great literary genius.*

Question: WHO IS THE LIVING PERSON YOU MOST ADMIRE?

Bill: *Without a second thought – my wife Lynn. This selection was not predicated on me staying in good favor to insure my rhubarb doesn't go to waste. Quite honestly, Lynn is the person to be admired for a myriad of reasons: first of which is for her faithful support and love over nearly 39 years of marriage to this type A+ personality of a husband; secondly, Lynn has helped to raise and encourage our wonderful and loving daughter (Melody) who emulate her mother's tradition in nourishing her own family in Helena, Montana. But without question, the greatest admiration of anyone I know today is in recognition of Lynn's positive, courageous and relentless spiritual strength of will as she battles Stage 4 metastasized breast cancer: and if the mountain of cancer survival wasn't enough for anyone to climb each day, Lynn continue to work cheerfully helping special needs and autistic children in the Pendleton School District to scale their own quality of life summit. She is a champion of the first degree.*

Question: WHAT IS YOUR PROUDEST ACCOMPLISHMENT?

Bill: *I guess I could say that opening for the Nitty Gritty Dirt Band and the Smothers Brothers during my college rock-n-roll (Eric Clapton wannabe) days. But realistically, that accomplishment can be cherished only for a moment. Organizing and getting the scarce resources needed to build a small hospital (mainly a birthing/pediatric center) in a hamlet outside of Hue, Vietnam, during 1967-68 is an accomplishment shared with fellow Seabees and Marines who made it possible as a lasting legacy to something other than just leaving behind the ravages of war.*

Question: WHAT IS THE MOST DIFFICULT CHALLENGE IN YOUR LIFE TODAY?

Bill: *The battle with cancer has been the most central challenge for both Lynn and me. However, the focus is on Lynn in maintaining a good quality of life during her ongoing intensive chemotherapy treatment. This is the most prevalent test faced today, but one that is a blessing to me for the privilege of serving as her caregiver.*

Question: WHAT DO YOUR FRIENDS CALL YOU?

Bill: *Grandma's choice = William; Aunt Myrtle's choice = Billy Lou.*

Question: HOW OLD ARE YOU?

Bill: *68*

Question: WHERE DO YOU LIVE?

Bill: *Pendleton, Oregon*

Question: WHAT DO YOU LIKE TO DO IN YOUR FREE TIME?

Bill: *Did someone say free time? Reading and writing are my relaxation sanctuary, but usually I find time only during the later evening hours.*

Question: IF YOU HAD TO LIVE IN ANOTHER COUNTRY FOR A YEAR, WHERE WOULD YOU LIVE?

Bill: *St. Germaine-des-Pres in Paris, France, along the romantic River Seine. This is a picturesque scene that remains unmarked by modern times, right out of the late Renaissance Period, with its cobblestones still intact, small shops, and a magnificent age-old cathedral second only to the grandeur of Notre Dame.*

It's a quintessential place where you can sit down to a table, immersed in another time, greeted by a friendly stranger to share a cup of espresso or coffee. Yes, this could only be a stay for a year as one would get real homesick for Pendleton's friendly espresso stands and cafes, and our own peaceful moments on the River Walk.

Question: IF YOU COULD CHANGE ONE THING IN YOUR COMMUNITY, WHAT WOULD IT BE?

Bill: *I would convert the Rivoli Theatre into a Performing Arts Center for local productions and author readings by Northwest writers.*

Question: TELL US ABOUT THE BEST BOOK YOU'VE READ RECENTLY.

Bill: *"A Dog's Purpose" by W. Bruce Cameron. This is a wonderfully narrated story from a dog's own internal voice that takes us on a soulful journey through its many lives to understand more clearly how to see and achieve our own individual purpose in life.*

Question: WHAT IS YOUR MOST PRIZED POSSESSION?

Bill: *I have a 58-year-old rare Gibson classical guitar that was a faithful companion during my early bachelor days making the rounds playing unplugged from one party to the next one, and at folk clubs as a troubadour of new folk songs (1960s style) and traditional ballads.*

Question: WHAT IS THE FUNNIEST THING THAT EVER HAPPENED TO YOU?

Bill: *I showed up a day early for the wedding of a friend having read the invitation wrong. I sat down in a pew at another wedding soon to begin. I looked around, and then whispered to a guy next to me, 'Gee, that's a different woman than who I thought Ed was going to marry.' 'Who's Ed?' Then I knew it was time to slip out quietly with my gift in hand.*

Question: WHAT IS THE ONE QUESTION WE DIDN'T ASK THAT YOU'D LIKE TO ANSWER?

Bill: *Have you ever met someone famous you always wanted to meet? Yes, and it was a 25 second lucky chance encounter that felt as if I was frozen in time and suspended within a daydream* *elevator ride. I've played an eclectic mix of music genres many years ago (rock 'n' roll, blues, folk, bluegrass, even classical choral works). However, it was the blues that captivated me the most, since I was a teenager, and it never let go since. I was heading up the elevator at Capitol Records in Los Angeles to the top floor to pick up master recording tapes for the music production company I was working with at the time (October 1984). Halfway up at the 5th floor, into the elevator stepped B.B. King, Dizzy Gillespie, and Herbie Hancock. Frozen in place, what do you say to three iconic blues/jazz master musicians without fear of looking like another starry-eyed fan, but still remain real cool, like I had arranged this little get together. With only a few fleeting seconds to the top of this unbelievable journey, I figured what the heck – one guitar place to the next, right? I blurted out what I had always wanted to know about B.B. King's unique guitar style: "Hey B.B., how do you bend those strings like you do to get that sweet 'painful feeling' sound?" He leaned forward with his signature big wide smile and booming voice, Well kid, if it hurts, you bend it until it gives into sweetness." With that shared bit of advice – one great musician to another (well, a wannabe), I knew I wasn't seen as just 'another goggling fan' hunting for an autograph. We hit the top floor with one more surprise. They invited me to sit in the engineer's booth and listen to some of their recording session. Well, I never did ask for their autographs. I gained something much more valuable and lasting about what separates the great musicians from the rest of us, as well as a personal lesson to live by.*

Today, Bill is at home doing his duty, caring for his wife in every way possible, as Lynn is terminal with cancer. Bill is also the official Master Gardener for the City of Pendleton, Oregon.

ONE OF MY BEST FRIENDS – HAROLD

This is a story about one of my very best friends. We grew up together and stayed in touch all our lives. I believe Harold only had two jobs his entire life. His first job was at our home town greenhouse, from an early age through high school. When we were in high school, we would get together with Tommy and a couple of other guys and go to the local dance at Valhalla near Lake Shetak. I remember one night after asking a couple of unfamiliar girls to dance, Harold said, 'Gee, I could slosh through the Johnson Rag better than through that tune." We were horrible dancers and a detriment to girls who would dance with us, but I guess we felt they were fair game. One night I got a date for the next Friday night dance. I went to pick her up and as I was about to knock on the front door, it opened and out came a bucket of bath water. I saw her younger brother being wiped down. The water just missed me so I thought the embarrassment would be too great so I left and she never knew. That's just the way things were in the 1940s.

After high school, Harold had a regular stint in the Marines as Corporal in the Marine Air Casual Squadron One. Then he went off to Macalester College and into the University of Minnesota, where he graduated with a degree in civil engineering. His second job was with Caterpillar Tractor Inc. for the rest of his working life. Harold accomplished a great deal working at Caterpillar, holding forty-three working patents including the two-piece sealed and lubricated master track link and, I believe, some sort of sealed bearing. So you can say that Caterpillar 'rolls' on Harold's inventions.

I went to see my good friend in Peoria, Illinois just before his death when he was terminal in a home. Harold was wearing his Marine cap. My friend Harold Reinsma was a great guy and married to a great gal Julie. He will be sorely missed by those who knew him best.

To all the young people thinking about what to do with your lives, take a page from Harold's life – if you have the ability, engineering is a very inspiring life to lead.

FROM MELVA TO LYLE

This story is from a lady who worked hard all of her life, and dedicated her life to all the principles that make a life worth living. When there were times that were not of the best, she always had her Christian background to fall back on.

I was born and raised on a farm about a half mile from a small town named Goodwin in South Dakota. We were a family of seven – a younger brother, three older brothers and two older sisters. We were a happy and caring family with each other, and my parents were strict, but something was lacking. Before I was born, my family went to the Baptist Church, but it closed from lack of members. I don't recall Mom and Dad talking about the bills, but I remember hearing Mom reading aloud after we were in bed, reading to Dad, and, in later years, I noticed her Bible was really worn, so that is when she must have been reading from it.

When I was in the fourth grade I noticed my classmates were always talking about Church and Sunday school, so I asked my best friend if I could go with her and she said yes. I started walking alone to her house every Sunday through two pastures and over three stoops (these were steep steps over fences). So we (my friend and I) wouldn't tear our clothes – we did more walking then into town. We always walked to and from school and even home at noon for dinner, if the weather permitted. I continued walking to Sunday school until I was baptized and confirmed. I had perfect attendance, and had the same teacher all the way through all classes. She was a great influence on me; I learned to love the Lord though I never heard about having a personal relationship with Jesus Christ. Soon after being confirmed, I started teaching Sunday School and later was Superintendent until I got married to Jim and moved thirty miles away from my home.

Jim had never been confirmed because his mother died when he was six years old. She also left a four year old sister and three brothers – ages eight, ten, and twelve. That ended Jim's church days until we were married. We both went to adult confirmation classes and I really learned more than before. Memorization was stressed and was a lot harder to understand in the King James version of the Bible.

We lived in an apartment in a small town and I was very lonely as the Church didn't take people in like they should have – they were all related. After a couple of years we were blessed with a baby girl, and later, another baby girl. When the weather permitted, I would put my two babies in the buggy and walk the four mile square. Later we moved to a farm and I had plenty to do and we loved it there. But, for three years our crops got burned out. We had plenty of machinery, but only bad luck. Jim was offered a job at Hyde Oil in Pipestone, MN. So we left our friends and off we went.

We joined the First Lutheran Church and I got more involved, which I had longed for. I was a trustee for three years – belonged to Circle and Aid, and went to a Bible Study every Wednesday night for years. It was there that I learned I had to accept Jesus Christ as my Lord and Savior – Lula Gilman was the Bible Study leader and I really learned from her. The Church Board called me three times to be the Treasurer and I always refused (never thinking to pray), but the fourth time they asked if I would fill in for Treasurer until December. The Lord seemed to say 'Go for it' so I took the job and loved it. I was afraid when the previous Treasurer came back that they would hire someone else as they promised, but they didn't, so I was Treasurer for six and a half years.

I started going to Christ the King Lutheran church and I was still Treasurer at the First Lutheran church. I didn't want to be a quitter in October, but I thought they would ask me to quit being I was not going to church there, but they didn't, so I finished the yearly books and resigned from the First Lutheran church at the January meeting. Those were hard meeting to go to as the air at times was cool.

When I resigned from the First Lutheran church, Duane Stratton called from Christ the King Lutheran church and asked if I would be Treasurer. There would be no pay, and that would be hard after receiving one for so long (at the First Lutheran church). Everyone was volunteering, but I was never sorry because we were such a happy bunch all working together. We all took turns cleaning the church and were called the Dust Busters.

In 1991 (the year my Jim died), when we were working on the budget, Chuck Schup asked where the Treasury was. I had to confess it had never been put on the budget when they started paying the secretaries and custodians, and I never had the nerve to say anything, so I wasn't paid for seven years, but I always loved this job. It was and is a real challenge. I enjoy working with the pastors and secretaries, and feel such a closeness with them that I have a hard time when they leave. I really enjoy the trustee meetings and I feel I'm gaining a lot of friends through this job. I've been Treasurer about thirty-one years.

I've always been embarrassed about this, but I don't recall what grade I was in when the Baptist church opened again and my family went there, but I just couldn't leave the Lutheran church and continued to go it alone.

Since I've lived in Pipestone, I've worked at Culligan, Madsen Drug, Pipestone Hospital Office, Fashion Tree, Pipestone Federal, and as Jim's bookkeeper at the Oil Company. I have two daughters, two sons-in-law, seven grandchildren, twelve great grandchildren, and one great great-grandson.

I've had ups and downs in life like most people do. I've had over twenty surgeries, mostly in my younger years. Jim was the healthy one until he got leukemia and died in 1991.

I began to tithe and I believe that wherever God leads you, He will give you what you need to get through; but what I find even more amazing about God are the extra blessings He surprises us with along the way.

Christ the King has been a real blessing to me.

Here is a little excerpt (so true to life) from a friend who was an officer in the Plumbing Union:

I leave you with this famous quote, "There are two kinds of people – those who do the work and those who take credit for it. Try to be in the first group, there is less competition."

FROM LUTHER C. ONKEN, SUPERINTENDENT, MURRAY COUNTY CENTRAL PUBLIC SCHOOLS TO LYLE

We are fortunate to have a school in our community. When you think of a town, usually the first thing that comes to mind is the school and what it is known for. We take pride in our school, the staff and students, and how they represent our community. Looking at what our District has to offer for its size, we have much to be proud of. This is a credit to the staff for their com-

mitment to student learning, and to students for their ability to understand the importance of quality education.

This District, along with many other small and rural communities, faces difficult challenges in serving the needs of children and public education. Historically, rural schools have offered unique benefits and attributes – for educators, students, and communities. The success of rural education is linked with what makes rural and small town America unique. The size of the communities contributes to the strong connection among rural schools, educators, parents and communities.

This Community as a whole has been supportive of how they value education. Rural communities depend on their schools to serve many functions beyond their primary mission of educating children. Rural school districts are often the largest single employer in their area and these schools serve as the social, recreational and cultural foundation for their communities. We should commend our staff, students and parents for how they value education.

I cannot emphasize enough the value of public education and the benefits of receiving a diploma or degree. When I think back on my own personal situation, I can attest to fact that without my education to rely on, I would not have been able to accomplish what I have today.

FROM JOHN T. TILBURY TO LYLE

Here are some quotes from students regarding their completion of training at Dunwoody that I thought might be of interest to some.

"Dunwoody was a great background for me. A day doesn't pass in manufacturing without me being reminded of my training at Dunwoody – the work ethic, the skills I learned, and the camaraderie of my Dunwoody family of friends."

~Jim Tilbury, 1974 (my relative - first cousin)

"I feel gratitude to Dunwoody for all that I have gained because Dunwoody was not afraid to take a chance with me, a poor uneducated Asian back in the days of WWII, where there was great prejudices against minority groups."

~Francis D. Yang, 1938

"Mastering each architectural segment required total dedication. Every month was a new segment and you had to successfully complete it before progressing to the next level. Students punched a time clock and instructors were strict about being on time."   ~Ann Fincham, 1979

"I cannot imagine what I would have been without my training at Dunwoody. I have used all that I have learned and beyond throughout my life."   ~Joseph Hillenbrand, 1949

I expect there may be more quotes from Dunwoody. Having gone through Dunwoody myself and spending a lifetime in the field as a journeyman pipefitter, I returned to Dunwoody for a visit at age 86 and found the school had advanced in every direction. Dunwoody now covers twenty plus work fields and, more importantly, its graduates have a higher percentage of job location than most other types of colleges.

* * *

In thinking about what you are and what your potential is, this is a personal thing. For myself, I never really gave it much thought. I just let it happen for the most part;, at least after going through Dunwoody Industrial Institute it seemed that way. You just figure it out. I never really worried about how to go about something. You just start thinking about the options and it more than likely will come out okay. I never totally concerned myself if there was some danger involved; I was too busy concentrating. It seemed natural to cope with the situation and that was all there was to it.

LINDA TOBIAS' STORIES TO LYLE

These are two stories from a very dear friend that had the courage to take control of her life when it seemed to be in shambles. Armed with her faith, conviction, and love of life, she conquered her medical problems and made a life worth living.

THINGS ARE NOT ALWAYS WHAT THEY SEEM by Linda Tobias

I work for a company that assists seniors to get needed medications, either with Medicare Part D plans or Patient Assistance Programs. I had a lady call and she was out of her pink pills. She didn't have money to buy any more and needed me to help her get her medication. I told her I needed to know the name of the medication and she told me it was pink, she didn't know the name. I asked if she had it in a bottle and she said yes. I asked her to get the bottle and read the name of the pill. After a couple of minutes she came back on the phone and I asked her if there was a label on the bottle. She said yes, and I said, can you spell it for me? She spelled m-a-y-o-n-n-a-i-s-e. I'm like thinking there is no medication with that name that I could find anywhere. I asked her again what the name on the bottle was and this time she got rather upset with me and screamed at me, "Lady, I told you it says 'May-On-Naise'." She said it was her pink pill...MAYONNAISE is what is on the label of the jar she keeps it in because she can't open the lid on her pill bottle that it was dispensed in. So she did just as I asked, I just didn't ask the right questions, I guess.

The Tunnel of Life

HOW A CITY PARK PICK UP BALL GAME CAN BE A LIFE CHANGER

by Linda Tobias

Back in 1970 in a small town in Southwest Minnesota that I grew up in, we were having a friendly summer baseball game at the park. I was the pitcher this particular day, and smack, I missed a line drive baseball that was hit right at my face. I ran home with a bloody nose and screaming with pain. After putting ice on it and getting the nose bleed to stop, life went on as usual, I thought. In the next few months I had increased headaches and trouble seeing the black board in school, so I made a trip to the eye doctor and glasses were needed; however, this didn't help much. I still had lots of issues with being able to see and the headaches. After going to the State Fair with the local high school band, and you know how kids are, they have to go to all the "free" stuff, there was a chiropractor booth at the fair and some of my friends and I went through. After an examination by a student from the Northwest College of Chiropractic in Minneapolis, he told me that I had some issues with my neck and I should consider going to a chiropractor to get checked out. Well, when I got home, my parents took me to a chiropractor in a neighboring town. After examination and x-rays I was adjusted and, much to my amazement, on the way home I was able to see really well. Needless to say, it was short-lived. After pursuing this issue, it was fond that I had 11 fractures in my face and cranial area from that baseball incident. By 1973 I was taking blind subjects in school to try to get my high school education completed. I continued with the chiropractic adjustments and was afforded some relief with the vision; however, it didn't seem to be something that was permanent. After a couple of years of continuing the battle with vision issues, it was determined there was an infection the facial bones that needed treatment. After doing the pre-

scribed treatment for the infection and my continued chiropractic adjustment, my vision settled down and with glasses I was able to see fairly well; however, the treatment for the infection raised issues with my liver and I was diagnosed with leukemia. I was told I would not see my 25th birthday. I did everything possible to go completely against what I was supposed to be doing and did it my own way. My chiropractor told me I had track shoes on and I needed to get them off and quit my running. After reaching an all-time low, and needing to go on dialysis, I decided I had two choices – I could go down quickly and not fight this, or I could try to make the best of a bad situation, put it in God's hands and see where it ended up. After much soul searching I came to a content place in my life. You know how we always kind of bargain with God? I vowed if I ever made it through this I would help others less fortunate than myself. Fast forward to 2012 – I am now 56 years old and am truly thankful for family and friends. I ended up by marrying my best friend, who happened to be my chiropractor. After 5 years of marriage, he was diagnosed with colon cancer and lost his battle in 5 short months. Because of his cancer journey and my cancer journey, I have dedicated myself to the Relay-for-Life of Murray County. I have served in various capacities with the organization from Co-chairman to Publicity. When you are faced with the reality of being told you will not see your 25th birthday, and somehow you fight through that battle and learn to lean on God, all things do become possible. I have tried to fashion my life by doing what I can for others. I have a saying that I try to live by when I think about friends – "Friends are angels who lift us up to our feet when our own wings have trouble remembering how to fly."

We all need friends, but, more importantly, we all need to be friends. The reward of doing for others is so much greater than the gift of receiving. It is far better to give than to receive.

The Tunnel of Life

* * *

This book is mostly advice to help teenagers secure a good life; and although I didn't want it to have a political flavor, unfortunately it cannot be entirely avoided. We have to change our political dynamics if we are to free up our youth to enjoy a complete and total lifestyle.

Let me first tell you what caused me to see how things are shaping out. I grew up in Slayton, Minnesota and then moved to California to find my dream. Since then, for a few years, I lived in Oregon and Colorado, only to return to California and then back to Slayton, Minnesota to supposedly finish out my life.

What I have seen is this. Minnesota has a large amount of farming. Several years ago a farm might have been eighty acres or more, but today there are no fences and most of the small farms are gone. One farm is as far as the eye can see, and the equipment (farm machinery) is huge, almost as big as a jumbo jet with the same electronic instrumentation.

I guess there is nothing wrong with this, but it means there is about one sixth as many farmers working today as there were in the past. My home town has the same population as it did sixty years ago. I came home to a town I didn't recognize. I went to church and there were about two dozen people attending. It used to be packed full and those who were there now were nearly my age – mid 80s. In five years will there be more than a dozen people in church? Where are the young people? I drove by one of the only two night spots in town and there were several more times as many cars in the parking lot than there are at church on Sunday.

Now, let's look at the other side of the picture - the political side. For nearly two centuries we have enjoyed life under the republic our forefathers created back in the late 1700s. It has not changed much in all those years in the way our country was run: but, in my opinion, we have "two cancers". No. 1 started about 1980 or so when Paul Volcker was in charge of the Federal Reserve and moving into George H.W. Bush's presidency, interest rates went out of sight. Then the Sarbanes-Oxley Act was passed. It stabilized banking procedures, but I believe the Act was repealed during the time of Allan Greenspan and President Bill Clinton. It was during this time that the banking industry began to unravel again until about 2005-2007, when it was at its worst, and it continues today under Ben Bernanke and President Barack Obama. Our present-day financial status is near collapse. The other cancer (No. 2), in my opinion, was started by President Clinton when he put his wife Hillary in charge of revamping the National Medical stance. Her attempts went on for about four years and finally Congress decided her plan was not adequate and it was not passed. However, "the Plan" didn't stop there. It went forward to President Obama's tenure. It seems to me that Hillary Clinton and President Obama probably put the present medical bill together over the years and got it passed in the first weeks of Obama's Presidency with a Congress of predominantly Democrats. The only thing is, this was not only a Medical Bill, but it had all kinds of other taxes and costs to the American public that had nothing to do with medical coverage. At that time, Speaker of the House Nancy Pelosi said "We have to pass it to see what's in it." This from a supposedly professional and intelligent politician? I always thought you studied a Bill, and then either passed it or junked it.

At this point I want to state what has been my greatest thought on politics – if, somehow, we could get a law passed that would require Congress to put only one subject matter on any bill, it would stop all special interest matters from being tacked on to some other type of bill. It would clean up Washington, D.C. in a minute. It is my guess that past Presidents and Congressmen are the worst offenders of this. At this point, Congress is almost unworkable, and the President seems to be sidestepping the Constitution, and nothing is being done about it.

Add to this the fact that our Judicial System is not in good shape. Look at the first O.J. Simpson trial or the John Boney trial (and many others) and the embezzlement which doesn't come out fairly: the people are always the losers. How can our young people ever survive in an environment like this?

It seems to me that the Clintons started to change this country into a socialist state, and it has really mushroomed under Barack Obama. He seemed to be blatantly open in his stand; for instance, he said on television that he was cutting off all border control money. This had a lot to do with the 60% favorable vote that put him in office for a second term. The cancer is now terminal.

Another piece of important legislation which I believe should take place is about court proceedings. It should be the law (to stabilize true facts) that all investigators or interviewers be required to tape record all interviews, so that later any final results and consequences cannot be perfected or redacted to meet a desired outcome. When I lived in

Colorado, my next door neighbor was Mexican. He was a good man, spoke fairly good English, and some of his family did also. One day we were in his back yard talking and he said, "Lyle, you have to learn Mexican."' I didn't answer that comment, but thought, am I hearing this right? This is the United States of America, but it's fast becoming the United States of Mexico.

Just before I moved back to Minnesota, we lived in Santa Ana, California for a short time. We lived in California three different times. This last time I was kind of shocked, because I found Santa Ana was 87% Latino. The City Council and the Mayor were all Latinos. I could hardly talk to most of my neighbors because of the language barrier, but they were, for the most part, good neighbors. The point is that this country in the last four years has practically changed from the Republic we knew into a Socialist State. What will happen in the next four years? I don't think this country will last another decade as we know it. What will happen to our children and our children's children?

We must take our heads out of the sand (not like ostriches) and look and see what is happening. We must take our country back by voting out those "career-congressmen", who have long since forgotten why they were sent to Washington (which was to do the people's work). If we don't get some new blood in Congress we deserve what is happening and what we will end up with. Our Constitution does matter and so do our children's futures. We are going bankrupt as a nation – both financially and morally. What will happen to our children? This should not be their fate.

This book would not be complete if I left out a comment on our three divisions of government. From a citizen's approach, we have an obligation to vote our conscience as well as with intelligence.

Now, having said that, why would we not consider voting out a few congressmen that have been in office for several terms and have long since forgotten the public they are supposed to represent.

This is where special interest begins to play out. They have to get all that money to run for office from somewhere and it doesn't come from fifteen or twenty dollars here and there from the general public. If we just vote out most long-term congressmen that seem to be adrift, I don't believe we would be wrong or stupid.

Now, about the President. Today it is very obvious our President is going outside of normal Executive power and sidestepping the Constitution. It is very obvious "it is my (*Obama's*) way or the highway." Where are Congress and the Supreme Court on this? Why should Congress get a black eye for doing its job? The media has too much effect on the outcome of congressional and political procedure. The President also has a power that should be toned down considerably...that of granting pardons. I think President Clinton may have pardoned more criminals than all prior Presidents put together. This is way out of order. People like Mark Rich, George Soros (and his money), and organizations seem to be bent on bringing the United States down. Companies like ACORN and many others seemingly exist to generate bogus votes for the Democratic Party. Where is the Supreme Court on this? They seem to be asleep most of the time.

The Supreme Court, in my opinion, is the weakest part of our government because the Justices are appointed instead of elected. This causes them to put a slant on most of their opinions or decisions as a result of which party put them in office.

They should have been elected by a "straight-away vote" of each and every citizen of the United States, not in the same fashion as the President (the Electoral College method).

In my lifetime, I recall only two politicians who said anything noteworthy or famous: President John Kennedy when he said, "Ask not what your country can do for you – ask what you can do for your country.", and President Ronald Reagan when he said, "Mr. Gorbachev, tear down this wall!" These statements were typical of those made by our founding fathers.

Patrick Henry also thought down this line when he said, "Give me freedom ... I know not what course others may take; but as for me, give me liberty or give me death!" He was talking about independence from English rule. He wanted a free country, and he would fight to the death for it.

These men and Presidents Lincoln, Washington, Adams and Jefferson are among the famously and truly dedicated individuals whose ideals and morals are missing from today's government.

I think back to when I was a young man; people had even then a more principled belief in government – life, liberty, and the pursuit of happiness. Today there is a more personal approach of 'what is there in it for me?' attitude. What will happen to our children?

I would sure like to know what goes through the minds of about 32 percent of U.S. citizens that seem to believe in and back everything President Obama does, no matter what he does. I often wonder if there would be any difference if our next President were Hillary Clinton. There is a lot of the Sahl Alinsky philosophy ("*12 Rules for Radicals*") floating around Washington these days. To me, it seems like there isn't any difference between Barack Hussein Obama, Hillary Clinton, and Russia's Vladimir Putin. You can't tell them apart.

Pogo (for those of us old enough to remember that cartoon character) may have been right when he said, "WE HAVE MET THE ENEMY AND THEY IS US!"

The Productive Years

I recently came across the following letter that has been aligned for quite some time with my own beliefs, and although it is not the scope of this book, it should have a substantial and meaningful effect on young people's thinking about their future well-being. I felt it would be a valuable inclusion to this book. It was written by a retired attorney, Don Heyer, to his sons on May 19, 2004.

THE WORLD SITUATION

Dear Tom, Kevin, Kirby, and Ted,

As your father, I believe I owe it to you to share some thoughts on the present world situation. We have, over the years, discussed a lot of important things, like going to college, getting jobs, and so forth. But this really takes precedence over any of those discussions. I hope this might give you a longer term perspective that fewer and fewer of my generation are left to speak to. To be sure you understand that this is not politically flavored, I will tell you that since Franklin D. Roosevelt, who led us through pre-and WWII (1933-1945) up to and including our present President, I have, without exception, supported our Presidents on all matters of international conflict. This would include (just to name a few in addition to President Roosevelt – WWII): President Truman – Korean War (1950); President Kennedy – Bay of Pigs (1961) and Vietnam (1961);[1] eight Presidents (5 Republicans and 4 Democrats) during the Cold War (1945-1991); and President Clinton's strikes on Bosnia (1995) and on Iraq (1998);[2] so be sure you read this as completely non-political or otherwise you will miss the point.

Our country is now facing the most serious threat to its existence, as we know it, that we have faced in your lifetime and mine (which includes WWII). The deadly seriousness is greatly compounded by the fact that there are very few of us who think we can possible lose this war and even fewer who realize what losing really means.

First, let's examine a few basics:

WHEN DID THE THREAT TO US START?

Many will say September 11, 2001. The answer as far as the United States is concerned is 1979 - 22 years prior to September 2001 – with the following attached on us: Iran US Embassy hostages - 1979; Beirut, Lebanon US Embassy – 1983; Beirut, Lebanon Marine Barracks – 1983; Lockerbie, Scotland Pan-Am flight to New York – 1988; the first New York World Trade Center attack (basement garage)– 1993; Dhahran, Saudi Arabia Khobar Towers Military complex – 1996; Nairobi, Kenya US Embassy – 1998; Dar es Salaam, Tanzania US Embassy – 1998; Aden, Yemen USS Cole (destroyer) – 2000; New York World Trade Center – 2001; and The Pentagon – 2001. (Note: During the period of 1981 to 2001, there were 7,581 terrorist attacks worldwide.)[3]

WHY WERE WE ATTACKED?

Envy of our position, our success, and our freedom. The attacks happened during the administrations of Presidents Carter, Reagan, Bush 1, Clinton, and Bush 2. We cannot fault either the Republicans or the Democrats as there were no provocations by any of the Presidents or their immediate predecessors, Presidents Ford or Carter.

WHO WERE THE ATTACKERS?

In each case of attacks on U.S., they were Muslims.

WHAT IS THE MUSLIM POPULATION OF THE WORLD?

25% [4]

ISN'T THE MUSLIM RELIGION PEACEFUL?

Hopefully, but that is really not material. There is no doubt that the predominantly Christian population of Germany was peaceful, but under the dictatorial leadership of Hitler (who was also Christian), that made no difference. You either went along with the administration or you were eliminated.

There were 5 to 6 million Christians killed by the Nazis for political reasons (including 7,000 Polish priests). (http://www.nazis.testimony.co.uk/7-a.htm). Thus, almost the same number of Christian were killed by the Nazis as the 6 million Holocaust Jews who were killed by them, and we seldom hear of anything other than the Jewish atrocities. Although Hitler kept the world focused on the Jews, he had no hesitancy about killing anyone who got in his way of exterminating the Jews or of taking over the world – German, Christian, or any other. Same with the Muslim terrorists. They focus the world on the U.S., but kill everyone in the way – their own people, the Spanish, French, or anyone else. The point here is that just like the peaceful Germans were of no protection to anyone from the Nazis, no matter how many peaceful Muslims there may be, they are no protection for us from the terrorist Muslim leaders and what they are fanatically bent on doing by their own pronouncements – killing all of us "infidels". I don't blame the peaceful Muslims. What would you do if the choice was shut up or die?

SO, WHO ARE WE AT WAR WITH?

There is no way we can honestly respond that it is anyone other than the Muslim terrorist. Trying to be politically correct and avoid verbalizing this conclusion can well be fatal. There is no way to win if you don't clearly recognize and articulate who you are fighting. So with that background, now to the two major questions:

1. Can we lose this war?

2. What does losing really mean?

If we are to win, we must clearly answer these two pivotal questions.

We can definitely lose this war, and as anomalous as it may sound, the major reason we can lose is that so many of us simply do not fathom the answer to the second question – What does losing mean? It would appear that a great many of us think that losing the war means hanging our heads, bringing the troops home, and going on about our business, like Post-Vietnam. This is as far from the truth as one can get.[5] What losing really means is:

We would no longer be the premier country in the world. The attacks will not subside, but rather will steadily increase.

Remember, they want us dead, not just quiet. If they had just wanted us quiet, they would not have produced an increasing series of attacks against us over the past 18 years. The plan was (and is) clearly to terrorist attack us until we are neutered and submissive to them.

We would, of course, have no future support from other nations for fear of reprisals and for the reason that they would see we are impotent and cannot help them.

They will pick off the other non-Muslim nations, one at a time.[6] It will be increasingly easier for them. They already hold Spain hostage.

It doesn't matter whether it was right or wrong for Spain to withdraw its troops from Iraq. Spain did it because the Muslim terrorists bombed their train and told them to withdraw the troops. Anything they want Spain to do, will be done. Spain is finished.

The next will probably be France. Our one hope on France is that they might see the light and realize that if we don't win, they are finished too; in that they can't resist the Muslim terrorists without us.

However, it may already be too late for France. France is already 20% Muslim and fading fast. See the article on the French condition by Tom Segel.

If we lose the war, our production, income, exports, and way of life will all vanish as we know them. After losing, who would trade or deal with us if they were threatened by the Muslims. If we can't stop the Muslims, how could anyone else? The Muslims fully know what is riding on this war and therefore are completely committed to winning at any cost.

We better know it too, and be likewise committed to winning at any cost.

Why do I go on at such lengths about the results of losing? Simple. Until we recognize the cost of losing, we cannot unite and really put 100% of our thoughts and efforts into winning. And it is going to take that 100% effort to win.

So, how can we lose the war? Again, the answer is simple. We can lose the war by imploding. That is, defeating ourselves by refusing to recognize the enemy and their purpose, and by really digging in and lending full support to the war effort.

If we are united, there is no way that we can lose. If we continue to be divided, there is no way that we can win.

Let me give you a few examples of how we simply don't comprehend the life and death seriousness of this situation.

President George W. Bush selects Norman Mineta as Secretary of Transportation. Although all of the terrorist attacks were committed by Muslim men between 17 to 40 years of age, Secretary Mineta refuses to allow profiling. Does that sound like we are taking this thing seriously?

This is war. For the duration, we are going to have to give up some of the civil rights we have become accustomed to. We had *better be prepared to lose some of our rights temporarily or we will most certainly lose all of them permanently. And don't worry that it is a slippery slope. We gave up plenty of civil rights during WWII and immediately restored them after the victory and, in fact, added many more since then.*

Do I blame President Bush or President Clinton before him? No. I blame us for blithely assuming we can maintain all of our political correctness and all of our civil rights during this conflict and have a clean, lawful, honorable war. None of those words apply to war. Get them out of your head

Some of us have gone so far out in our criticism of the war and/or our administration that it almost seems they would literally like to see us lose. I hasten to add that this isn't because they are disloyal. It is because they just don't recognize what losing means. Nevertheless, that conduct gives the impression to the enemy that we are divided and weakening. It concerns our friends, and it does great damage to our cause.

Of more recent vintage, the uproar fuelled by the politicians and media regarding the treatment of some prisoners of war perhaps exemplifies best what I am saying. We have recently had an issue involving the treatment of a few Muslim prisoners of war by a small group of our military police. These are the type prisoners who just a few months ago were throwing their own people off buildings, cutting off their hands, cutting out their tongues, and otherwise murdering their own people, just for disagreeing with Saddam Hussein. And just a few years ago, these same type prisoners chemically killed 400,000 of their own people for the same reason. They are also the same type enemy fighters who recently were burning Americans and dragging their charred corpses through the streets of Iraq. And still more recently, the same type enemies were and are providing videos to all news sources internationally of the beheading of an American prisoner they held. Compare this with some of our press and politicians who for several days have thought and talked about nothing else but the "humiliating" of some Muslim prisoners – not burning them, not dragging their charred corpses through the streets, not beheading them, but "humiliating" them. CAN THIS BE FOR REAL? The politicians and pundits have even talked of impeachment of the Secretary of Defense. If this doesn't show the complete lack of comprehension and understanding of the seriousness of the enemy we are fighting, the life and death struggle we are in, and the disastrous results of losing this war, NOTHING CAN.

To bring our country to a virtual political standstill over this prisoner issue makes us look like Nero playing his fiddle as Rome burned – totally oblivious to what is going on in the real world. Neither we, nor any other country, CAN SURVIVE THIS INTERNAL STRIFE. Again I say, this does not mean that some of our politicians or media people are disloyal. It simply means they are absolutely oblivious to the magnitude of the situation we are in and into which the Muslim terrorists have been pushing us for many years. Remember, the Muslim terrorists' stated goal is to kill all infidels. That translates into ALL non-Muslims – not just the United States, but throughout the whole world. We are the last bastion of defense.

We have been criticized for many years as being 'arrogant'. That charge is valid in at least one respect. We are arrogant in that we believe that we are so good, powerful, and smart that we can win the hearts and minds of all those who attack us, and that with both hands tied behind our backs we can defeat anything bad in the world. The fact is: WE CAN'T!

If we don't recognize this, our nation as we know it will not survive, and no other country in the world will survive if we are defeated.

And finally, name any predominantly Muslim country throughout the world that would allow freedom of speech, freedom of thought, freedom of religion, freedom of the press, equal rights of anyone (let alone everyone), equal status or any status for women, or that has been productive in one single way that contributes to the good of the world.

This has been a long way of saying that we must be united on this war or we will be equated in the history books to the self-inflicted fall of the Roman Empire. If, that is, the Muslim leaders will allow history books to be written or read.

If we don't win this war RIGHT NOW, keep a close eye on how the Muslims take over France in the next five years or so. They will continue to increase the Muslim population of France and continue to encroach little by little on the established French tradition. The French will be fighting among themselves over what should or should not be done, which will continue to weaken them and keep them from any united resolve. (Author Note: Doesn't that sound eerily familiar? I must make the following comment. THIS IS EXACTLY WHAT RUSSIA IS DOING TO THE UKRAINE RIGHT NOW!)

Democracies don't have their freedoms taken away from them by some external military force. Instead, they give their freedoms away, politically correct piece by politically correct piece. And they are giving those freedoms away to those who have shown, world-wide, that they abhor freedom and will not apply it to you or even to themselves, once they are in power.

They have universally shown that when they have taken over, they then start brutally killing each other over who will be the few who control the masses. Will we ever stop hearing from the politically correct about the "peaceful Muslims"?

I close on a hopeful note, by repeating what I said above. If we are united, there is no way that we can lose. I believe that af-

ter the election, the factions in our country will begin to focus on the critical situation we are in and will unite to save our country. It is your future we are talking about. Do whatever you can to preserve it. Love, Dad

ADDENDUMS TO THE FOREGOING LETTER

[1] *By the way, on Vietnam the emotions are still so high that it is really not possible to discuss it; however, I think President Kennedy was correct. He felt there was a communist threat from China, Russia, and North Vietnam to take over that whole area. Also, remember we were in a Cold War with Russia. I frankly think Kennedy's plan worked and kept that total communist control out, but try telling that to anyone now. It just isn't politically correct to say so. Historians will answer this after cool-headed research, when the people closest to it are all gone.*

[2] *As you know, I am a strong President Bush supporter and will vote for him. However, if Senator Kerry is elected, I will fully support him on all matters of international conflict, just as I have supported all Presidents in the past.*

[3] *Stats source http://www.infoplease.com/A0001454.html.*

[4] *The Institute of Islamic Information and Education (www.iile.net/Inti/PopStats.html)*

[5] *"I don't think the Army or any branch of service runs any type of war anymore. It's done by senators and congressmen. There are too many civilians involved." Returning Iraq veteran, Sgt. 1st Class Greg Klees as quoted in the Cedar Rapids, IA Gazette on May 13, 2004.*

[6] *There are 64 Muslim countries. This number does not include countries like Spain that are already controlled by Muslim terrorists.*

(Author Note: After reading this letter, I refer to the Benghazi, Libya incident. The changing of the talking points by our government leaders was made so as not to incite more terrorist attacks, and as a reason for not taking steps to protect the Consulate. Does this seem like we are coming together to fight terrorism? And it would seem the Obama Administration is a complete reversal of all previous Presidents and their administrations. I believe also that the Benghazi incident is just one of the more recent terrorist attacks on the United States. Will we win this war?)

THE MANY CHAPTERS OF LIFE

I would like to look at life's actions for a moment and paint two pictures.

When you finish high school (if you get that far), you should have a very basic or rude understanding of what life is all about. Hopefully you will have enough understanding of basic mathematics, chemistry, biology, physics, English, history, and some social skills to function on your own – that is, outside of your parents' 'hood of protection'. At this point you either make something of yourself (by yourself) without the protection of parents or you fail to have much of an existence at all.

First Picture- Those that go on in life to achieve higher education and accomplish the pinnacle of success, and have a social and productive life also go forward in two directions. Most of them are valuable assets to society (in addition to their own benefit) as teachers, engineers, or researchers, etc.: others will use their education and skills in ways that steal from society, such as computer hackers, embezzlers, and some politicians who benefit themselves at the expense of the general public without rhyme or reason.

Other Picture – Those who leave high school may also go in one of two directions. (1) They may get some form of directional training such as beautician or some sort of mechanic, learn to master a cash register or provide some form or type of unskilled service to get life means or income. Then there are those that leave high school and, at this point, (2) if you are one of these and you don't have more than one or two friends, you have not learned any social skills at all and will probably remain at home long under your parents' protective shell and become so dependent upon them that you cannot function at all in society.

Now these two directions ahead are plain and simply described.

But, in addition to these problems, we all have to put up with killers, rapists, and just plain mean people who are, in general, at the lower end of society.

Then there are those at the higher end (and I describe them in this fashion): what society needs is protection from predators like some lawyers, judges, politicians, and some corrupt business entities.

In summing this up, I sincerely hope and believe there are more honorable people with good intentions out there than there are unscrupulous ones in society, but the good may be losing the battle. So what is next?

I guess all you have, as an individual in this world, is the love of life you can muster by yourself, your self-respect, and however many friends you attract.

The United States, in some respects, may be the kindest country there is, but too much is slanted against you for all the wrong reasons.

"Our judicial system only protects the powerful." Bill O'Reilly was also right when he said, "Our Supreme Court Justices are not pro-active. They are like lizards sunning on a rock – they don't move unless something comes along."

Congress won't get off their dead butts and do anything that helps the general public, probably because the Lawyer Lobby in this country is so powerful.

My advice is that any way you can perceive a life of peace and prosperity, take it to the bank; because, for the most part, you are on your own. Live a life of compassion and be kind; but, above all, be honest with yourself, work hard, and, for God's sake, try to stay out of the way of any issues that may provoke the need for a lawyer, because you will be the loser either way.

JUDITH BAXTER TO LYLE

I felt this book needed the input of a serious grandma, and I saw this lady whom I thought might fill the bill. She was in a store with her little granddaughter and they were having a ball looking at all the Halloween stuff. I asked her for her suggestions for a good life, and the following is what she offered.

THOUGHTS AND VALUES THAT I LEARNED FROM INFANCY TO SIXTY-FIVE YEARS OF AGE

All these years, I've used positive thinking and tried to be the best I can be. Showing and being honest with oneself and with others builds confidence and draws others to identify with and most likely to be in one's association.

While growing up, all my personal decisions have been based on knowing oneself and being just that, no matter what others are doing or thinking. Perseverance of one's conscious decisions, foremost and consistent, sometimes quietly and other times not so quietly, depending on who and how aggressive those are who are confronting and questioning. Of course, when it comes to how decisions affect only me, my position starts with "this is what I think" or "this is how I feel". Then I follow through on this decision.

In other situations which might include a group decision, I state my position and see what the vote produces, and I can change my mind with what others had to say, again keeping the above philosophy in mind.

My experience with this philosophy has taken me into decades of integrity for myself and others, and the understanding of others who do trust and show their respect, whether or not they believe the same.

Just remember, you can achieve your full potential, make up your mind and go for it!

THIS IS THE FIRST DAY OF THE REST OF YOUR LIFE

Think about that! Anyone in their late teen years should approach their future slowly enough to consider all avenues. We ALL make mistakes, but this is not the time to rush into a direction in life without good reason, especially because of pressure from a bad situation or from someone else's desire or circumstances. A lofty goal is not delusional by any means, but think it over and be honest with yourself. Nothing in life is free. It takes a lot of hard work and effort to get anywhere that is worth being there; however, that is what will make all those many years ahead of you worth living and so very valuable – not the nightmare that they could be. Possibly a teacher may have said something that would set you thinking. Listen to that one person in your life that stands out and would have your best interests at heart.

Some young people may have had a devastating time in their lives early on, and have little help for the future, so direction for them may be hard to find. But, it is out there and you (and they) can find it for yourselves.

There are so many endeavors out there to pick from. Consider the medical field. There are the many types of doctors (i.e. internists, pediatricians, general practitioners, urologists, psychologists, etc.). The same goes for nurses, research and laboratory technicians, engineers, science and literary research, business law, and endeavors in the varied fields of the arts – music, art, literature, poetry, theatre, dance, etc.

You can notice a person's demeanor and know if they are a happy camper in their lives and endeavors.

For a moment, let's take off our colored glasses and see life as it really is. When you were a baby, you were taken care of; basically, the only thing you did was eat, sleep, and relieve yourself. When you start to grow up in the learning years, it's up to you how life will shake out. Will you possibly be a garbage hauler? Maybe an electrician, or maybe a doctor or lawyer? If you go through high school and just sit there in class, never do your homework, go home and get a soda and watch television or play games on the computer, you may end up a garbage hauler. Now, as such, you can support yourself and a family, but not very satisfactorily. It wouldn't be the best life. If you decide to become an electrician, it will require a more dedicated effort on your part to learn all the functions of electricity. You cannot make mistakes when dealing with electricity. You will have a better life of security and satisfaction. If you become a doctor, lawyer, chemist, school teacher, or engineer, you will put forth a lot more energy, time, and money preparing yourself for these professions, but the rewards will be much greater. The point is you have to make up your mind early in life if you are going to be a success and to what extent. Are you going to be lazy or curious?

Personally, I feel that all life efforts should be meaningful in nature. That said, I believe that eventually too much lawyering and politicking will be our Nemesis. If you disagree with this comment, just look at what has happened in the past. To begin with, our forefathers established this country on certain principles, along with a Christian basis that has stood for over 200 years; however, some erosion has happened in recent years. Just look at the facts. The Ten Commandments were rejected and ejected (eliminated) from all public buildings for whatever reason. It is not acceptable now to say 'Merry Christmas'. It is politically correct to say only 'Happy Holidays'. Well, Christmas would not be the event it is if Jesus Christ had not been born – there would not be any Happy Holiday season. How stupid do they (whoever they are) think we are? How long will it be before 'In God We Trust' is removed from our currency? English has always been the spoken language of this country. About seven years ago another bill was introduced in Congress to make English the sole official language of the United States (the previous bill for the same purpose was made in 1981 by Senator Hayakawa from California. It did not pass.) I went to a local library and had them bring up the vote on their computer. There were thirty-two Democratic senators who voted against the bill (if my memory is correct), and they included Hillary Clinton, Barack Hussein Obama, and John Kerry. I didn't find out how many Senators didn't vote at all.

It is my hope that we are causing our teenagers to realize that if their future success is to have any form of great accomplishment, peace of mind, and serenity, they have to accept the fact that life begins with a lot of hard work on their part, and they need to stay informed of what our politicians also are up to. It has a great bearing on their future well-being.

* * *

The following story comes from a teenager with her heart set on being a writer, and from the story she has written she seems politically motivated, but that is what young people do, strike out in every direction.

My name is Carolyn. I am very grateful for the opportunity to have my opinions heard. I am 16 years old. I've never been too involved or interested in the political aspects of this world. Lately though, economical concerns, global affairs, and government-related events seem to have forced themselves into my life and attention. Every time I turn on the news, I hear of changes trying to be made in our country. Each proposed law and bill seem very complicated, with technicalities and rules that I do not understand. Step back though, and view as a whole the law or bill that the government is trying so persistently to approve. Behind all the useless paperwork, conferences, and fine print, what is the government really trying to do? Simplify the whole plan and look at the possible outcome. Weight up the positive and negative effect this could have on our society. Nine times out of ten, I am finding that the people in charge of our country don't have the

*best interests of America's residents in mind. To me the govern-
ment comes off as an evil, greedy group of people given way too
much power. The group of elected officials running the United
States today has drifted far from what our government was originally intended to be. Motivated by self-interest and personal
gain only, these people are ready and willing to accept bribes, to
make false and misleading promises to millions of people, and
fight so adamantly for a bill that is unfair and unnecessary. The
Health Care Reform Bill is an extremely controversial topic. I
will admit I do not know the details of this plan. All I know is
that the government pushed so hard for this bill to get passed and
it was accepted. Now many of the government officials that got it
passed do not want to be a part of the aftermath. People who voted in favor of this reform bill don't want their own families to be
included in the effects of this bill. This worries me because these
people obviously know about something in relation to this bill
that the majority of America does not. The unfair and greedy
minds of people with such authority are what concern me the
most. In elementary school, children are taught to treat people
how they, themselves, wish to be treated. The powerful people in
this country truly seem to have forgotten that policy. All people
have opinions, feelings, thoughts, and dreams. No one life is
more valuable or important than another. The group of people
dictating the United States of America comes off like they don't
care whose life they affect as long as they get a paycheck. They
blatantly do not care, and this is wrong. There are over 300 million people in this country, and that number is steadily increasing. The young mother working two jobs to support her children
and the old couple retired on a farm somewhere in Pennsylvania
are the people that make America the beautiful country it is.
Children playing hopscotch on sidewalks and young adults jog-
ging with their dogs give the United States its unique personali-*

ty. This innocent image is being rapidly diluted by the people in Washington, DC, trying to drive this place into a troubled, unfair excuse for a country. Here's where (being 16 and unable to boast a thought) in-depth education about politics works against me. I can only express my dreams about how I wish the country was, and voice my fears of the future, as a member of the generation that will be left to clean up whatever mess the government makes today. I cannot propose a big grand plan of action that will save the day, nor can I really make a huge difference at the present time. But I certainly hope the adults of America today can take into consideration the opinion of my generation and do something to keep the United States of America from falling into a dangerous pit that we don't know how to get out of.

* * *

This is a story of the life of a teenager who lived a life of hell during his Formative Years, brought on by his father who thought more of his own personal image that anything else. This boy was kicked out of his home by his father for all the wrong reasons, but he found a life worth living on his own, helped by his mother's prior influence.

Are there not many things or gestures that can be used to squelch a young boy's self-esteem more than constant belittlement, and harassment towards his mother? And (my opinion) beatings more severe than the crime committed warranted? Looking up to your father should be an inspiration in a boy's Formative Years growing up. It is sorely disappointing to not see this happen and so detrimental to his future. IT IS NOT ALL SUGAR AND SPICE growing up in a supposedly "Christian home". Ha! Ha! Instead of "Jesus Loves Me...", it was "how can you do such a thing", "you will amount to nothing but a long-haired do-nothing bum!" This from a member of the church choir, who was in charge of the Sunday School Department, and an all-around good Christian guy. Again I say Ha! How many kids do you know that actually make plans to run away from home in the fifth grade (10 or 11 years old) simply from the fear of receiving a whipping because you had a 'D' on your report car. Needless to say, some things never change, except for the beatings. One other thing, some of the behavior I myself have acquired: negative attitudes, very smart mouth, use of profanity, and very little regard for any type of authority, whether it be personal or legal. My mother passed away in 1982 at 43 years of age. She was and still is my positive influence. I can't imagine how upsetting it must have been for her to see such disturbing things towards her children. My mother had tremendous love and care, and portrayed a true sense of Christian ethics. Moms are (in my opinion) so under-valued in today's standards. If it had not been for my mother's examples of goodness, kindness, humility and outright generosity towards others, I don't think I would have ever experienced these characteristics in others. When the passage of time prevails, not through the elements of patience, maturity, and obvious healing, wonderful easing of pain can be achieved. Understanding, love, and compassion can be expressed and shared with siblings, neighbors, personal friends, co-workers, etc. The need for kindness cannot be ignored. Countless times, calls for help have come to me in waves of continual support, and the attitude behind their motives – completely selfless friendships – for me have not come in waiting arms, but more in the mind set of 'whatever you sow, that shall you also reap (KJV Gal 6:7). Unfortunately this does not work favorably all of the time. There have been huge disappointments along the way, but some have led eventually to some helpful insights on how to deal with other issues. Fifty-four years of acquiring experience and an ever-increasing desire to see what God has in store for me around eve-

ry waiting corner is my daily driving source. I'm observing how much fear, hurt, hatred, and disrespect is in the world. My desire is that I may be a blessing to someone today.

* * *

The following is something I found that may be worth thinking about.

FOR ALL THOSE BORN BEFORE 1945 – WE ARE SURVIVORS!!! Consider the changes we have witnessed.

We were before radar, credit cards, split atoms, laser beams and ballpoint pens; before pantyhose, dishwashers, clothes dryers, electric blankets, air conditioning, drip-dry clothes, and before anyone walked on the moon.

We got married first and then lived together. How quaint can you be?

In our time, closets were for clothes; not for coming out of... Bunnies were small rabbits and rabbits were not Volkswagens. A meaningful relationship meant getting along well with our cousins.

We thought fast food was what you ate during Lent, and Outer Space was somewhere on earth.

We were before house-husbands, gay rights, computer-dating, dual careers and commuter marriages.

We were before day-care centers, group therapy and nursing homes.

We never heard of FM radio, tape decks, electric type-writers, artificial hearts, word processors, yogurt, and guys wearing earrings. For us, time-sharing meant togetherness – not computers or condominiums; a "chip" meant a piece of wood: hardware meant hardware. And software wasn't even a word!

In 1940, "Made in Japan" meant junk and the term "making out" referred to how well you did on your exams. Pizzas, McDonalds, and instant coffee were unheard of.

We hit the scene when there were 5 & 10 cent stores, where you bought things for five and ten cents; Sanders or Wilsons sold ice cream cones for a nickel or a dime. For a nickel you could ride a street car, make a phone call, buy a Coke or buy enough stamps to mail one letter and two post cards. You could buy a new Chevy Coupe for $600, but who could afford one?

A pity, too, for gas was 11 cents a gallon and the attendant not only pumped it for you, but he cleaned your windshield, checked your oil and water, and put air in your tires at no charge (and usually with a smile).

In our day, cigarette smoking was fashionable, grass was mowed, coke was a cold carbonated drink and pot was something you cooked in. Rock music was a grandma's lullaby and aids were helpers in the principal's office.

We were certainly not before the difference between the sexes was discovered but we were surely before the sex changes. We made do with what we had, and we were the last generation that was so dumb as to think you needed a husband to have a baby!

No wonder we are so confused and there is such a generation gap today!

BUT WE SURVIVED!!! WHAT BETTER REASON TO CELEBRATE!

In addition to this, my thoughts are about the freedoms people had in those times. Yes, they all worked hard and got along without many of the pleasures and conveniences we have today, but I truly feel they, in general, were much happier and more relaxed mentally than we are today.

We have a greater tax burden today, more restrictions to our everyday lives. I guess you would call that less freedom, with more concern and much more complication in life. The only out is more education to cope with it all, but GOVERNMENT is doing its share to dumb us all down.

Today, if you don't have a higher education, your future will be that of a third world country; and that is what the United States is rapidly becoming.

* * *

This is a very interesting and accurate accounting of recent times. I came across this article a while back when I was living in Oregon, and I believe the situation has only gotten worse.

The essay was written seven years ago by a judge in Charleston, South Carolina, who prefers anonymity, and who was alarmed at trends weakening the foundations of society, such as life styles, morals, standards, outlook on life, patriotism, self-respect, independence, and spirit.

NIGHTMARE

"I am living in a nightmare, whence I cannot awaken." WELCOME TO MY NIGHTMARE.

This is the land of the free and home of the brave. Whisper the truth in this brave, free land, and they call you a bigot. Suggest the obvious and you are a fascist. WELCOME TO MY NIGHTMARE.

We give cash money, free medical services, food stamps, free housing and utility subsidies to the lowest class of society, as payment for producing welfare babies, usually illegitimate. Those who pay the taxes for these services – the workers – must first pay their taxes and then pay retail. Welfare mothers make money by making babies; taxpayers cannot afford children. WELCOME TO MY NIGHTMARE.

Everyone can do everything as well as anyone else, whether they can or not. If the test results prove otherwise, change the test. We no longer value equality of opportunity, but rather equality of results. Equality of opportunity means that some will fail; therefore, boost up all those who might fail, even though now no one may succeed. WELCOME TO MY NIGHTMARE.

Jobs, scholarships and federal contracts go firs to minorities, then to the most qualified. Women are minority, even though they are not. Irish, British, French, Germans, Polish, Swedes, Danes, Italians and Jews are not minorities, even though they are. We must now discriminate in favor of minority children and grandchildren, and against other children and grandchildren, in the name of justice. WELCOME TO MY NIGHTMARE.

Lawyers and judges control every facet of our lives, public and private. No one is safe from a lawsuit, no matter how ridiculous or frivolous. Policemen cannot arrest, teachers cannot teach, and bureaucrats cannot administer without fear they will soon answer to somebody's lawyer, for some half-forgotten mistake. So in many cases, they do nothing at all, out of fear of lawyers. WELCOME TO MY NIGHTMARE.

The leaders of our news media hate their own country. They see only evil in America, only reason and clarity in those who would destroy her. It is far better for Americans to be killed, than to kill. It is far better for America to lose a war than to win, better still to refuse to fight at all. WELCOME TO MY NIGHTMARE.

Criminals control our streets, our stores, and our homes. We respond by installing brighter street lamps, expensive burglar *alarms, and heavier locks. Every criminal is given probation or released after serving a small portion of his sentence, regardless of the crime. He returns to the street to rape and maim again, and society's leaders blame society for making him what he is.* WELCOME TO MY NIGHTMARE.

Sexual perversion has been abolished. Nothing is perverted; all is individual choice. If you protest, you are a Nazi. WELCOME TO MY NIGHTMARE.

You may speak these words privately, because everyone knows they are true. You may not speak them publicly, because then you are intolerant; you despise the poor; and you smile upon oppression. One must not speak the truth. One must be open, sensitive, enlightened. The land of the free and the home of the brave has become the land of the feeble and the home of the craven. We adore freedom of speech, but do not dare use it. Use it, and we will punish you. WELCOME TO MY NIGHTMARE.

It would seem this Administration has only made this nightmare worse. WELCOME TO YOUR CHILDREN'S NIGHTMARE.

* * *

This is a little personal advice I feel should be basic. To those young people fortunate enough to have been given sensible guidance and who have great expectations (like entering the research field or something equally important), you, first of all, have the direction, the will, and hopefully the means to achieve your goal along with the ability to get there. That being said, you are put in the position of keeping that goal clean. By that, I mean you must live a life of reputable existence to go along with that position. I refer to the issues of becoming a lawyer; far too many of them fail in the reputable existence, which should come with the position in life that it **commands**, but doesn't necessarily **demand**. People, in general, have a great respect for and expect more from people in high positions. They look up to them for security and the future well-being of mankind. Hopefully more of the masses will reach these same high goals too, but we all need someone to look up to and trust – this makes us all better people. Any position in life which doesn't command and receive trust from the masses is no position at all.

FROM DAWN AT HER MOTHER ESTHER RUTH'S FUNERAL ON MAY 25, 2012

Anyone that knows me knows that I am never speechless. In fact, I usually have a lot to say and am often the one that is asked to sing at these events.

My Mom is probably quite unhappy with the fact that I am not singing for her today, but I know she understands that I cannot do it. She always understood everything. If I was able to sing today, my musical choice would be "I'm Everything I Am Because You Loved Me". The fact that you did love me so deeply and so perfectly is the reason why I am rendered speechless and voiceless today.

The entire family was asked to speak, but my brother said it all with his reply of "we all want to, but none of us can."

I have been lucky enough in my life to have four true heroes. Everyone should be as fortunate as I am to have their Mom counted as one of them. Some of you had her as a teacher, some as a co-worker, some as a friend, but I got her wisdom and guidance in everything important about life. For me, she was the pure definition of LOVE. She always gave more than she received, never expected anything in return, and quietly accepted any personal injustice brought her way.

The Tunnel of Life

It is difficult to talk about my Mom as a separate person from my Dad. They are one and somehow formed the perfect union of two lives.

As a little girl, I watched Fairy Tales and often wondered what happened in the "They lived happily ever after" part of the story. As an adult, I am still searching for the happily ever after, but as a child, I was privileged to live in their happily ever after world. Disney spent an entire life trying to offer the happiness to others that my parents effortlessly created in our home.

Children and family were the cornerstone of Mom's life...again how lucky my brother and I were to be part of her world.

There are so very many stories and memories to share, but I will briefly leave you with a true "Mom" story that represents how she supported me as a daughter.

Anything – and I mean anything – I did in life was possible because I knew Mom (and Dad) loved me and were there to catch me if I fell. It didn't matter if I was a success or a failure in my mind, my Mom would always tell me, "You are so good at that." I would look at her and say, "But you are good at that too." Her final words were always, "But you are so much better."

During a time in my life when I was struggling with whether or not I was a good Mom, she was there. When I doubted myself, she gave me the stern German voice that was reserved for moments when she was going to make a point and it would not be argued with. She firmly said, "You are a good Mom." I wanted to say, "If I can be only half the Mom you are, I will count myself successful", but there were no further words that day.

So today, I say to you: Mom. You have created and left a legacy of Love through your children, your grandchildren, and the many lives you have touched.

"Mom – I Love You – and – YOU are SO much better!"

* * *

The following story comes from a young man that has his life on track today and success is definitely in his future. I had very little time to get 'Fred's' story and there were a few loose ends.

Fred's life started to unravel quite early in his life. His parents were divorced, so Fred was living with his mother. She paid little attention to him so he was on his own and could do pretty much whatever he wanted. By the time Fred was in his early teens, he had fallen into bad company. Drinking and fighting was a way of life; he thought that was what everyone did. As time went on, his mother could no longer handle their situation, so Fred went to live with his father. Life didn't change at all. Fred's father, for the most part, lived just outside the law – very clandestine and devious. One day Fred came home and it was apparent that he had been in a bad fight, as he showed plenty of signs of suffering. Fred's dad commented, "Did you win the fight?" Fred said yes, and his dad said "Good! If you hadn't won, I would have beaten you myself." As time went on, one day Fred's dad gave him a car. The only problem was that his dad had stolen the car. It was lucky for Fred that the car never came into the picture as a problem or Fred would have been in jail. One day Fred and his dad were out somewhere and they ran into three guys that knew Fred's dad. They were looking for him because he had swindled them on some deal. A fight was inevitable and Fred's dad told him to stay out of it, "You're too young for these guys." As the fight went on, one of the men took out a revolver and pointed it at Fred first – point blank – just to let him know he should stay put, then he swung around and shot Fred's dad in the forehead, killing him instantly. The men all left quickly and Fred was left there standing dazed and shocked. This was where Fred was heading if he didn't change his ways.

When I first met Fred, he had turned his life around. He went through high school and got a job with a large facility as a security guard (complete with carrying a weapon). At this first meeting, I noticed his fine demeanor and I approached him with a request for his story for my book. He said yes, but he never seemed to find the time. One day when we got together, he poured his story out to me quite unexpectedly, so I had to put it together. I found out that Fred was unhappy with his job; he needed one with better pay. I told him about my Local Union and how I felt he would be a perfect candidate. Fred met with the Union, but the time frame for the next Union classes had already started, so he enrolled in night courses at a junior college until he could start the next year with the Union courses. I know Fred's life is on track today.

FROM EDDIE TO LYLE

This story about a teacher pretty much covers his whole life.

For seven or eight years of my elementary school days, I was never a real student. I didn't even care, because I didn't think anyone else cared. I would come and go as I pleased. When I entered seventh grade, I found out something – the teacher saw all of us as individuals. It wasn't just about the smart and rich anymore. If you stood out, you were accepted. I started to get self-worth; I even had some teachers whom I thought liked me.

Later on in high school, I was the only one left living at home and my mother needed my help. I was so busy working to pay the household bills; I never really knew what I could do. I learned to support myself by necessity if nothing else; I babysat, mowed lawns, helped farmers, and worked numerous other jobs. Thank God I grew up fast; it kept some people off my back. Ray Short carried me through the winter and I paid the oil heating bill with the next summer's work.

I was told to forget about college. That didn't set well with me, so I decided to do the impossible. I could hardly pay the bills, let alone go to any higher education. I will say here that my father taught me independence and my mother instilled honesty in me. If I had my life to live over, I could never leave out my Army days. It was then that I got to test all my Sunday school lessons, and put some of my philosophy of life together. The Army also gave me financial support so I could achieve college.

I never got an "A" until I went to college – what a feeling – what a wait; then real meaning came into my life, a wife and then family. Discussion time again – what do I want to be or do? What a wife! She helped me on this situation and many more – this is called TRUST. *She may be little, but "Oh My!!!" I thought I wanted to be an optometrist, but it was out of our financial picture. I turned instead to a life of teaching. There I found all the money I would ever need, and something that cannot be taken to the bank. I was never sorry that I became a teacher. Kids are everything. I look back at my life and feel that I gave it my all, and that it meant value to all of those students. I feel very happy with myself. Life has been good.*

FROM DEBBIE TO LYLE
GRACE-FILLED LIVING

John 1: 1-13

The Tunnel of Life

Most of you know that I am no accomplished musician. I have a son who is; a daughter-in-law who is more than a passable musician; and even young Chloe (my grand-daughter) at age 5 is carrying a fair tune – but I am best at enjoying music. I have had the pleasure, however, in the last 34 years of serving congregations with wonderful musicians – including this one. And they have taught me a thing or two about their craft.

One of the things they have taught is that a good musician "embellishes" music to make a composition more attractive. Sometimes, in fact, you can find a little "grace-note" woven into the music – not a principal note in the piece, but a quick little trill or turn that comes unexpectedly, giving joy and life to the musical piece.

Well, there are grace notes in music and there are grace notes in life. There are experiences that break into the humdrum of daily existence.

For example, as a young mom, I recall that one of my sons was known for breaking into my study when I would be writing: whirling around the room, giving a quick hug around whatever part of my being his arms could reach, and quickly darting out again. How I wish that "6 ft. 2 in. strapping grace note" of a guy would whirl in more often now.

So it is! Grace notes are fleeting! Beautiful moments come when we least expect them and from unlikely sources!

As much as we might like to do so, we cannot write grace notes into our own lives. Grace is a gift from "...God, who became flesh and dwelt among us." God's Spirit blows where it will. The tragedy for most of us, however, is not that we cannot write such notes, but that we fail to hear the many grace notes God continually sends us. It is so easy to get caught up in what we deem to be important tasks that we fail to be sensitive to our surroundings or to one another.

David Heetland, a professor at the seminary Gary and I attended, conducted an experiment several years ago. Several of us were invited to preach on the parable of the Good Samaritan as a class assignment. Each week, however, as we were route to class, we were detained by a professor until just moments before it was time to preach. So we had to hurry to get to class lest we be locked out of the class. On the way to class, though – nearly tardy – each of us came upon a person, clearly in distress, who requested our help. Guess what? Most of the seminarians passed by without stopping in order that they might get to Preaching Class to preach about the Good Samaritan.

How easy it is to get caught up in our own lives and miss the opportunity to be a grace-note is someone's life.

A father, writing to his daughter, suggested that the willingness to be open, to trust, to approach others in freedom is perhaps the greatest contribution we can make to the world. What beautiful words from a father to a daughter – or for those of us who seek to live the Christian faith. For it is through sensitivity, openness, and willingness to allow God to speak to us whenever, wherever, and from whomever, that we discover grace (not after grace) notes and learn that much of life can be sheer sacrament. Mother Teresa expressed this powerfully in her prayer "Jesus my Patient":

DEAREST LORD: MAY I SEE YOU TODAY AND EVERY DAY IN THE PERSON OF YOUR SICK. WHILST NURSING THEM, MAY I MINISTER TO YOU. THOUGH YOU HIDE YOURSELF BEHIND THE UNATTRACTIVE DISGUISE OF THE IRRITABLE, THE EXACTING, THE UNREASONABLE, MAY I STILL RECOGNIZE YOU, AND SAY: 'JESUS, MY PATIENT, HOW SWEET IT IS TO SERVE YOU. LORD, GIVE ME THIS SEEING FAITH, THEN MY WORK WILL NEVER BE MONOTONOUS.' AMEN.

Grace notes abound!

David Heetland, to whom I referred earlier, is Vice President of Garrett-Evangelical Theological Seminary in Evanston, Illinois and has kept a diary of all of the visits he has made in the course of a normal week on behalf of the seminary. Note the grace! The first call David made in a particular week was to an elderly widow in Wisconsin. On that day, David did not come away with a gift for the seminary, but he came away with something far more valuable – a gift of understanding. As he listened to this elderly widow, he gained new understanding of sacrificial, joyful giving. Here was a woman who lived very frugally – saving the rest in order to give it away. She shared with David how she had decided to give up drinking coffee so that she would be able to give more to a hunger project she cared deeply about. She devoted hours each day to volunteer work: visiting shut-ins, doing hospital calling, delivering church newsletters.

Did this all add up to a rather mundane existence? Not in the least! This same woman began chasing butterflies in her 70s. She became a world expert on Monarch Butterflies and was able to speak enthusiastically about raising them, tagging them, and researching them. She concluded her visit with David by remarking that God had taught her about life through Monarch Butterflies.

This Vice President of Development from a prestigious seminary thought to himself, 'How much God has taught me through you.'

Many of us share a common gene pool. Others of you choose to marry into that common gene pool. It isn't pure and it isn't perfect – but it is (sorry) DeVine!

And, just as many of us have large brown eyes, and dark hair with a glint of red when seen in the sun, a good sense of humor, and – unfortunately - vivid memories of past hurts and grudges

– we also share remarkable men and women who gave much to the world. It is something to celebrate!

May we also live in such a way that our lives become grace notes for others, and may we experience each day the everlasting grace that comes only from our Lord and Savior, Jesus Christ. Amen? Amen!

FROM JEANNINE TO LYLE
COLLECTIONS

When I was a young girl, I was what my mother called a "hoarder". I would call myself more of a "collector" who never threw anything away. I liked everything that was cute or sparkly; such as porcelain figures, blown glass animals, trinket boxes, stuffed animals, rocks, and plastic Breyer horses.

From an early age, my mother would nag me about cleaning out my room and throwing away the "junk" I wasn't using. I just couldn't do it.

I was always very frugal and thought that I might need these items someday. She would accuse me of being just like her mother who was a total "pack-rat" who would keep even the elastic straps from old bras.

As I grew into a young woman, I began collecting items to fill my future home. I had a love for antiques, "Gone With the Wind" movie memorabilia, carousel horse figurines, Norman Rockwell creations, and pink Depression glass dishes. After I turned 21, I started to travel and wanted to start a collection of items to remember the adventures and the places I had visited. I was still very frugal, so what would be the smallest and least expensive trinket? Shot glasses! They were easy to find, easy to pack, and I could use them for mixing drinks back home.

At the age of 25, I married my husband, Brian. We shared a love of antiques and Victorian houses. He introduced me to the appreciation of wine. As we visited the many vineyards and tasting rooms of California, I began to realize that it would be a better idea to collect wineglasses from the places we visited. We enjoyed having our friends over for wine tasting parties and these glasses were quite useful.

After I turned 30, we moved to Washington State, the home of Starbucks coffee. Neither Brian nor I were coffee drinkers at the time, but after many years, many jobs, many children (actually only 2 children, but it seemed like 10), and many late nights, we succumbed to the temptation and have picked up quite a habit.

Now that I am almost 50, our vacations are mainly now trips to visit family in other states. We use those moments to see as much of the different regions of the United States as possible. It seems like the natural progression of my life is to collect, you guessed it, coffee mugs. We now have an entire cupboard full of stoneware coffee mugs and plastic travel mugs we picked up while traveling through places such as Yellowstone National Park or visiting our son at Washington State University. Brian and I fight over our favorite mugs; whoever turns the pot on first, get their choice.

I still have most of the collected treasures from my life. I do have a hard time parting with things.

It is funny to reflect on how my collections have changed over the years. Looking back I can see that my priorities were changing at the same time. My kids don't want my little trinkets, and hate our antiques. I think I'll keep these anyway in case they change their minds.

FROM ALYSSA SNYDER TO LYLE

Sometimes people will discover a direction or interest early in life and just follow it to fruition. They are the fortunate ones, but this can happen to you also. While you are in high school or even before, you should be on the lookout for such an opportunity when you see it. This is what happened to this professional person.

Many times I get asked the question "How did you decide you wanted to become an eye doctor?" I smile to myself thinking back to my middle school science fair project on the human eye. As a pre-teen, I doubt that I realized my destiny at that point. As I grew more mature, my interest in the eye care field became more concrete. I worked at Shopko as a customer service representative, so I approached the optical manager about working as an optician. After my on-the-job training was completed, I was able to pre-test patients before seeing the optometrist, assist patients in picking out and ordering glasses, and adjusting frames. Soon after starting my part-time job as an optician, I began my undergraduate education at a public school. As a freshman, I was assigned to a "pre-optometry" advisor who later became my chemistry professor. I met with him once a semester to make sure I was taking the right classes to get into optometry school. He encouraged me to get a business degree in addition to my prerequisite classes for optometry. After doing a little research on my own, I found that I could apply to optometry school as a junior instead of as a senior, as long as the prerequisite classes were complete. I was ecstatic, one less year of college, I could forget about my business degree and just focus on my science classes! Filled with excitement, I went to meet with my advisor. He told me "you will only be accepted as a junior if you can walk on water." Most students would continue their education at that point and apply as seniors – but not *me. I was a very determined young woman, wanting to prove my advisor wrong. I applied and had two interviews: one at Ferris University in Michigan and one at Pacific University in Oregon. My supportive parents accompanied me to the interviews. I was rejected at Ferris and*

133

accepted at Pacific. Optometry school wasn't easy. I was a small town farm girl from half-way across the country. I missed many weddings, graduations, and other special events, but optometry was important to me, and I was committed to it.

I now work in a private practice in rural Minnesota. I would never have gotten to this point unless I was aggressive about following my dream. I continued on even when others told me it wasn't do-able; I had the support of my family, and most importantly, I was a determined, stubborn young woman who was 100% committed to my dream of becoming an optometrist. Believe in yourself even when others don't, and where there is a will, there is a way.

* * *

The following story requires an in-depth medical information approach. It is a story from an elderly man about his gay son, and since this is a book about all walks of life, this one is as real as any. I asked for advice from the medical field to be sure my book was accurate. I learned that the medical profession has established knowledge markers to represent the depth of research on any medical problem, and to establish the theory or fact status. A #1 marker has an established association in the medical field and a #4 marker has an established association, but needs more research to understand its position. DNA was recognized not very long ago and we don't know what is just around the corner. At any rate, being gay has a #4 marker at the present time. I wanted to be sure there was medical feasance (the performance of an act), so here is this man's story.

The man said that in many ways, it was a day he grew up a little more himself, even at his elderly age. He said his son came to him one day when he (his son) was about twenty-five, and said, "I have something I want to discuss with you and mom. I should have done this years ago, I guess, but at this point in my life, I have to get on with my life. I don't know any other way to say this except 'I am gay!' I don't know how you two feel about this except..." In some place about here, I spared our son and said, "Don't let this bother you, we love you and that is all that matters." His mother and I proceeded to assure our son that nothing of importance had changed and his probity was the important thing. He was very relieved and said this was the hardest thing he ever did in his life – to tell us this. Our son had carried this burdensome secret for roughly thirteen years, while joining with all the other children; but, all at once in adolescence, discovered he didn't agree with the rest of the world and the general train of thought of most young people. He realized he was different, but didn't know why. He kept it to himself and learned to live with it. He learned to maintain outward normalcy through his own skill and intelligence. It was only through his abilities that he achieved healthy, constructive high school years, and went on to be one of the youngest people to graduate from a university at one point below the Honor Roll. In itself, this did not mean anything to him, but to do well in his own eyes was important. If he hadn't been working so much to make it easier on us, he undoubtedly would have made that "B" an "A". The point is, he did not go downhill into a negative life style or oblivion when he realized he was different. Later, when we thought through his situation, we realized he had been horribly deprived. He never could enjoy teenage life or have a normal relationship with girls like 90% of his male friends could (and did). He will never come to us and say 'Mom and Dad, this is the girl I want to marry and go through life with', and receive our blessings. The only association that can be placed on this life style is 'partner'. There isn't a specific word to describe this type of union like 'marriage'. He will never have children of his own, see them grow up, or see their accomplishments. He will not have children to be proud of, or to be proud of him. All of his hard work, accomplishments, and college education are almost a waste. It will stay this way until medical science finds out why and how to correct the imbalance in genes that causes this kind of life that our son and so many others are coping with.

Being gay is not a disease, but it may be a chemical or genetic imbalance. We don't know enough about it yet, but it can be equated with the biblical trials of lepers and leprosy. There again, they didn't know what the reason was for their affliction and those with it were shunned. Our problem is the lead weight in our hearts; knowing we could not be there for him in all those years of secrecy. How lonely those years must have been. In my mind, he is one of the greatest people alive. He said it was hard to comprehend when he first put a handle on his "affliction". I can't imagine living with this all those years and keeping sane. No person should ever have to go through this anymore. Mankind has got to wake up.

* * *

The following story gives you a feeling of pride and satisfaction over what one young man, Taylor De Ley, has done so far.

His life's accomplishments are just beginning and the path he will cut in life is unimaginable. It also leaves you with the thought, if he can do it, why can't you? Taylor is young, just seventeen, but he is inspiring. This young man from Yorba Linda, California flew around the perimeter of the United States. Taylor set out on July 9th in an experimental plane that he built with the help of his father. He and his RV-4 plane landed in seventy-nine airports in thirty-six states, spending seventy-two hours in the air and traveling twelve thousand seventy-four miles. Taylor did this before he was legally old enough to rent a car, so at each stopover, there had to be someone available to chauffeur him to hotels or wherever he could freshen up for the next day. (Of course, the trip was all laid out for these accommodations.) At one stop, he landed at Johnson Creek in the mountains of northern Idaho and camped overnight with another pilot who is a friend of his. The tent he used was part of the 100 pounds of baggage Taylor could stow in his plane, and it was used on more than one occasion. He took pictures on a fly-by at Daytona Beach on his way to Cape Canaveral and Key West, Florida. He stayed with friends along the way at many stops, including El Paso, Texas. He flew by the Space Needle in Seattle, Washington, and Kitty Hawk, North Carolina, where he landed at the site where the Wright brothers experimented with gliders and made their first powered flight at Kill Devil Hill. It had to be exciting to view the different places of the United States from eight thousand feet up.

I talked with Taylor De Ley once about giving me a story for this book, but he was too busy to give me the time. (His mother said she would help me if I couldn't do it on my own.) I understand now that Taylor plans to complete college in a couple of years or so (less than the usual 4-years). That seems impossible now, but I am sure he will just add knowledge, training and experience to his present capabilities; and then, for him, there will be no limit to what is possible. All things are possible if you have the training first. Without proper training, you will just CRASH.

Chapter Four

The Golden Years

By this time in life you should have learned patience, which should help you to enjoy the rest of your life. These are the years when you will probably do all the things you wanted to do but didn't accomplish in the Productive Years; you could not get away, it didn't seem like the best use of the money, or whatever. You travel, do personal things like tackling the computer (if you haven't already), write a book, take up golfing, or maybe just do what your spouse wants to do for a change. This is also a time when you may find a split in the road through the tunnel of life. Taking one path, some people just go into their houses and never come out or do anything. Their bodies soon deteriorate in one way or another, and it is a sad ending. The other path, in most cases, is as busy as life was before, but in special ways. It is a time to reminisce. You have the time to enjoy life and can get satisfaction in helping others or just communicating with others. One word of advice however - with all your wisdom, don't try to run other peoples' lives.

Some people feel the Golden Years are not all that golden, but I think they try to run the Golden Years into the next phase of the tunnel of life.

In the Productive Years (when you reached them), you had no alternative but to go ahead. Father Time was pushing you down the tunnel of life, but when you reached retirement, you found yourself somewhat in the Twilight Zone for what to do next. For years you had "...your nose to the grindstone, your shoulder to the wheel, your finger on the pulse, your eye on the ball and your ear to the ground." (Proverbs) There wasn't much time to plan for retirement, but here you are – you get up in the morning and there is no rush, no deadline, no confusion, just calm and lots of time. Everyone else has gone to work. It's quiet. That is until your brain starts to work and then there is lots to do, but no organization or schedules to meet. These are not necessary. You are retired and you can find all kinds of projects to do. You wonder if you will live long enough to complete them all.

I found that writing this book was a great experience. It put me in contact with a great many people whom I never would have met otherwise. In the challenge of putting it all together, I couldn't help seeing the wide range of life styles that exist. I have put people in four classes of endeavor. First let me say as we all start to grow up in the learning years and on into life, we pick and choose what really makes us tick. That said, the first group covers most of mankind. This group has some semblance of moral conviction and finds life to be a co-existence of peace and posterity. They understand and appreciate most of what surround us. The second group consists of those who seem to put a high priority on fortune and, in their wildest dreams, fame. If they have a moral foundation, life is quite complete. The third group is one I could never quite understand. These people never find any basis in life and that is probably because of poor parenting. They find it easy to blame others for everything that happens to them – their misfortunes and their failures. The fourth group is, for lack of a better term, the nerds. These people seem to not need all of the grounding or bases that the first group lives by, and they seem to have a more singular reason for life's direction. We really could not survive as well as we do without the nerd, because, in their genius, mankind does need and is improved by the nerd's accomplishments. We just seem to be on another page from them – marching to a different drummer.

When I thought about my intentions for this book, I met with many people and explained my thoughts to them. If their responses or comments seemed worthy, I asked them if they wanted to put some inspiring message in my book about their lives that would set teenagers to thinking, "Maybe I'll try that!" The overall response was that they were excited and thought the book to be a great idea. One of the first comments was "I want to read it when it comes out." Some people offered to write something, but, as it turned out, few followed through with their promises. So I guess I must do more writing and hope my thoughts are true to nature. I think some people go through life like a piece of wood floating down the stream (aimlessly, without guidance), and others are like a boat being steered down the stream (on stream, with controlled aims and goals).

FROM RAY TO LYLE
ON AGING PARENTS

Caring for an aging parent is a responsibility few people ever expect or envision. However, I was raised with the model of bringing elderly family into the home. After my father passed away, my mother relocated to Mexico to care for her aging mother. My grandmother lived to the age of 96. I knew the time had come where my mom would move in with me. It is a task that is filled with personal sacrifices and rewards.

My mother moved in with me weeks after my grandmother's passing. I decided it would be best to sell my townhouse and purchase a home to better accommodate my new living situation. I purchased a home near my brother so he could assist me with the care of our mother.

I quickly learned that I was alone in this endeavor. I have had little to no assistance from any of my sibling. Initially, it was upsetting, but I have come to find this challenge to be rewarding.

My mother battled breast cancer and I am happy to report that she won the fight. It was difficult to see her go through extensive chemotherapy and radiation treatments. She looked frail and weak, but refused to give up. She insisted on doing everyday housework despite how she felt. It was heartbreaking to see her without hair, and know she would soon be facing a mastectomy.

My mom is still with me at the age of 75. Her decline has been slow, but I can see the subtle changes. It is a blessing to have her with me. That's not to say it hasn't been work. I realize the time I have with her is finite and losing her terrifies me. I don't want to have any lingering "if only..." thoughts when she is gone. Caring for my mother has certainly made my life busier and more complicated. But I wouldn't have it any other way.

The real challenge is still yet to come as my mother continues to decline and will require day to day or even minute to minute attention. I trust in the proverb that says, "Life does not put things in front of you that you are unable to handle."

HINDSIGHT – SOMETHING TO THINK ABOUT

Riding in an ambulance in the winter during a storm, the snow was starting to drift across the road and, to make matters worse, it was after 8:00 pm at night and it would be almost a two hour trip from our small town to a hospital in a bigger city. I wasn't sure if my heart was my immediate concern or if the ambulance tipping over and going into the ditch was. It was kind of like riding a horse or being on an air flight in bad weather, just bouncing around – what would it be like if I had a broken hip or such? At any rate the thought went through my mine "hindsight". If I had taken better care of my body, mainly eating a healthy diet, maybe I wouldn't be taking this trip. Besides that, there was all the discomfort of going through all the tests and finally the operation put in stents, to say nothing of the cost when you get well and see the bill for it all. My point is to take care of your body early in life or you end up like me. You don't need a 32 oz. cola with that greasy hamburger and largest french-fry order every day – just once a week (or less - once a month?) would be measurably better. A little advice to all of you who have retired and have too much time on your hands: All that pie, cake, candy, and cookies will do you in, in nothing flat. Think about it, you probably have many good years ahead of you – why not take advantage of them – and you won't look like a barrel either.

RECOGNIZING A STROKE

Some people that suffer a stroke stay with us today. Some don't die; instead, they end up in a hopeless condition. (It only takes a minute to read the following.)

A neurologist has said that if he can get to a stroke victim within 3 hours, he can **totally** reverse the effects of a stroke. He said the trick is to get a stroke recognized, diagnosed, and then get the patient medically cared for within three hours - which is tough.

Thank God for the sense to remember the **3** steps: **S T R!** Read on and learn.

Sometimes the symptoms of a stroke are difficult to identify; unfortunately, this lack of awareness may spell disaster. The stroke victim may suffer severe brain damage if bystanders fail to recognize the symptoms of a stroke. Doctors today say a bystander can recognize a stroke by asking three simple questions:

S – Ask the individual to **S**mile.

T – Ask the person to **T**alk – to speak a simple sentence. (i.e. It is sunny out today.)

R – Ask him or her to **R**aise BOTH ARMS.

Note: Another sign of a stroke is this: Ask the person to stick out their tongue. If the tongue is crooked, if it goes to one side or the other, this is also an indication of a stroke. If he or she has trouble with ANY ONE of these tasks (**S T R** or **Tongue**), call 911 immediately!!! And describe the symptoms to the dispatcher.

This message could save many lives in the future.

COMMENTS FROM MY GOLDEN YEARS

The Golden Years

This is a little human interest story about WWII. I didn't fight in that war, but would have gladly. I fell in between that war and the Korean War in age, so my army time was in Korea, but before that war actually started. Some of my classmates quit school and enlisted, and some had to lie about their age. We didn't know how long the war would last, but I wanted to finish school first. The thought here is – we were all very patriotic in those day. I, like so many people, followed the war in the newspapers, and on the radio. We were aware of the death and sorrow from those who did come back in part. There were so many lives lost and the pain goes on for a lifetime for those left behind. There are parts of those years that had their better moments; for instance, some of the greatest music ever written came from that time – music that stood the test of time such as George Gershwin's *Rhapsody in Blue* and *Ebb Tide*. This music helped make that time more memorable for all those who fought in that war and returned to our country to enjoy it. After the war, as a result of the war effort, we experienced an increase in many comforts, and major advancements in everything from cars to medicine. There was something good that came from all that bad (war). I often think of those whom I knew from my home town that didn't come back from the war. Even though I had not necessarily associated with them, I did know of them. In the end I just felt proud to be a United States citizen. We all did know how to be appreciative in those days.

I feel the need to mention my own observations about things surrounding our everyday life that we don't seem to take seriously enough. Sine WWII, the United States has been the stabilizer for the world (more or less), and it was definitely a major reason for the outcome of that war. For the past 65 plus years we could have used nuclear weapons or germ warfare (or whatever is in that Pandora's Box), but we didn't, because we were not after world domination. However, there is at least one threat to world sanity which may soon rear its ugly head – *Sharia* law. If *Sharia* law and nuclear weapons ever come together, it would be DOOMSDAY. This is definitely something to think about. Some years back I wrote an editorial about North Korea (back when we were unaware of the Arab world problems. I called North Korea the cradle of hate with their obsession with nuclear weapons, but now it seems the cradle of hate is concentrated in the Arab world. What bothers me is that our politicians are willing to live in ideology and "kick-the-can" down the road in their culture of corruption, and do not worry about any threats this late in the game. We follow these same politicians and their dogma by putting them back in office over and over. I frequently think we are all "NUTS"!!!

One thing older people might do is give the younger generation advice from their older experiences, including what is the true nature of things - just facts, no polishing, no putting a slant on anything – just the plain, unvarnished truth. If the younger generation is receptive, giving them an approach to see through bias or ideology might allow them to at least vote intelligently.

Our Country has always been about free speech and opportunity. This was because of people like George Washington, Thomas Jefferson, John Adams, Benjamin Franklin, and Alexander Hamilton who, among our many other forefathers, had the courage, insight, and depth of mind along with great suffering, to create this great Country. It has also been a Country of great definition. Proof is evident in the way people flock to the United States from everywhere on the globe. This makes me think that by all logic and reason, our young people should be able to mature with healthy bodies, minds, and souls to accomplish anything they have a will to do. Our unique concept of life, liberty, and pursuit of happiness stands somewhat alone in the world. A look back in time is confirmation of this. Look at all the improvements to life we have achieved, including a man on the moon (not that we accomplished all this alone, but we were a major participant). All this ingenuity should inspire our youth in many ways, not make them feel intimidated by past generations. Our children, just like us, are the future. They are the heirs of the first revolution in this Country that created the United States, and, God willing, not the last heirs.

Having said that, it is my opinion there is a conspiracy now going on. Looking back at over two hundred years of this country's existence, it was still coming together (and hardly had a firm footing), when Aaron Burr, in the early 1800s, encouraged a separation of part of the U.S. from the Union. Because he supported this separation, he was accused of being the American "CATILINE". (Lucius Sergius Catilina, Roman politician, was considered responsible for almost destroying the Roman Empire at the time of Cicero 63-62 BC.) During Lincoln's time, the South and the North had an American CATILINE situation, but the Union survived. Now the Union is facing another American CATILINE. In just over four years this country has changed from what it was for over 200 years (a "nation under God") into a Socialist government with a worldly or cosmopolitan foundation rather than a religious one. God Help Us! What will happen to our children?

* * *

Unfortunately, I was unable to get more stories from different walks of life for this book, but I didn't want to wait any longer. I felt it was time to get this book on the market. The sooner the right people read it, the more lives can be changed. This is all I have ever really wanted.

I didn't want it to be political, but there was no way of getting away from politics. Our young people have to know how eroded our government has become. It will be their problem to solve by making the necessary changes to correct it.

We are in a time we have been in before, when this new country had a Tea Party and dumped all the English tea in the harbor. Yes, at that time, the people had enough of English rule and taxation without representation. Now, we are in a similar situation with 18 TRILLION DOLLARS of debt; only this time we are being forced from a democracy into a communist regime by way of a socialist state. Not only that, but the believers of Muslim *Sharia* law have vowed to put their flag over Washington, DC.

I have said before, there isn't a great deal of difference between the Republicans and Democrats of our two-party government system, but will the new Tea Party movement in the Republican Party possibly change the party and clean it up? It would seem that the powers that be in the Democratic Party are mostly nefarious and pernicious, and there is no-one willing to "clean up THEIR act." So, what will happen to our children?

FOUNDING FATHERS

Since I have made several references in this book to our Founding Fathers, I would like to acknowledge them all, including the following with a special recognition. These men, including those who inspired them, were all intricately involved with the formation of this country by their special intellectual desires, drives and strengths.

They include George Washington, Benjamin Franklin, John Adams, Thomas Jefferson, John Jay, Alexander Hamilton, Thomas Paine, James Madison, John Hancock, Samuel Adams, Patrick Henry, Gouverneur Morris, and John Quincy Adams. We, as citizens, have a responsibility to honor and carry forth the principles they promoted and defended.

GEORGE WASHINGTON was Commander in Chief of the Continental Army during the American Revolutionary War. He was unanimously chosen by electors as the first President of the United States for two terms in 1788 and 1792. In 1787 Washington presided over the convention that drafted the United States Constitution. He was the first to be called the "Father of His Country".

BENJAMIN FRANKLIN helped write the Constitution of the United States. During the American Revolution, he convinced the French to help the Americans. Franklin told the French that if the British won the war they would be too powerful. He signed the Declaration of Independence, the Constitution, the Treaty of Alliance with France, and the Treaty of Paris, 1783.

JOHN ADAMS was a delegate to the First and Second Continental Congress. He was the first Vice President of the United States and the second President of the United States. In 1783, after the Revolutionary War, John Adams helped write the peace treaty with England. It was called the Treaty of Paris. His son was John Quincy Adams, sixth President of the United States.

THOMAS JEFFERSON was the principal author of the Declaration of Independence. At the beginning of the American Revolution, he served in the Continental Congress. He was the first Secretary of State under President George Washington. While serving as the third President of the United States, he oversaw the acquisition of the Louisiana Territory in 1803.

JOHN JAY was a diplomat, and the first Chief Justice of the United States Supreme Court (1789-95). Jay was the Governor of New York State (1795-1801), where he became the state's leading opponent of slavery. His first two attempts to end slavery in New York in 1777 and 1785 failed, but a third attempt in 1799 succeeded.

ALEXANDER HAMILTON fought in the Revolutionary War and became Chief of Staff to General George Washington. He was a major author of the Federalist Papers, and was also a delegate to the Constitutional Convention. Hamilton was the United States' first Secretary of the Treasury. He was an advisor to several Presidents and one of the most prestigious attorneys in Manhattan, NY.

THOMAS PAINE has been called The Father of the American Revolution. In 1776 he anonymously published a book called "Common Sense". It inspired the American people to want their independence from England. He wrote that the country should become a Democracy and that Americans could govern themselves rather than be governed by a King (at this time, George III).

JAMES MADISON helped frame the Bill of Rights. Madison made a major contribution to the ratification of the Constitution by writing the Federalist Papers along with Alexander Hamilton and John Jay. In later years, after being elected the fourth President of the United States, he was often referred to as the "Father of the Constitution."

JOHN HANCOCK was involved in revolutionary politics and joined with Samuel Adams to carry out the Boston Tea Party. Hancock was elected President of the Second Continental Congress. On July 4, 1776, he signed his name on the Declaration of Independence so large that King George III could read it without his glasses.

SAM ADAMS wrote letters about independence and sent them to newspapers and leaders around the country; but he signed all the letters with different names (other than his own) so that people reading the papers would think all of Boston wanted independence from England. He led protests against the Stamp Act and helped advance the Revolution by organizing the Boston Tea Party.

PATRICK HENRY signed the Constitution but worked hard to have the first ten amendments (The Bill of Rights) added. Henry protested the Stamp Act and was one of the first radicals for American Revolution. He was an orator, and is most famous for his speech for independence, "...but as for me, Give me Liberty or Give me Death!"

GOUVERNEUR MORRIS has been called the "Penman of the Constitution". He wrote the Preamble to the Constitution with Thomas Jefferson; he edited the document; and he signed the Articles of Confederation. In an era when most Americans thought of themselves as citizens of their respective states, Morris advanced the idea of being a citizen of a single Union of States (The United States of America).

JOHN QUINCY ADAMS was significant for his time as Secretary of State in the Monroe Administration. He was instrumental in improving relations with Great Britain, and, he was a strong supporter of the Monroe Doctrine, which helped limit European involvement in the affairs of the Western Hemisphere. Before election as President in 1824, he served as U.S. Minister to the Netherlands, Prussia, Russia, and Great Britain. He was the first President to advocate federal support for internal improvements, and the only President to serve as a U.S. Representative for 17 yrs. after his Presidency.

FROM KEVIN TO LYLE

My name is Kevin DeVine. I am 22 years old and have just started my first year of professional school working towards a doctorate in pharmacology. I am an Eagle Scout, was president of my high school class, and just recently got engaged to the most wonderful woman ever. I have been so blessed throughout my life, and it has not been by my own strength.

In life, many times we focus on ourselves and our strengths and weaknesses because it's easier. We know ourselves, sometimes painfully well, and, for the most part, we know our limits. We feel like we have to have it all figured out, and create who we want to be. Let me tell you though, the measure of what you can do is so much more than what you can do alone. I have absolutely no doubt that I would not be the person I am today without friends, family, and God.

Working from the bottom up, it is important to have friends. Not the most friends, not the most popular friends, but friends who want to be a part of your life and will invest in you. These are the types of friends who will help you with anything life throws at you. When you have a decision to make and you don't know what to choose, they can help and offer wisdom. They can also reach down and help you up. If your own strength in any matter is failing, having someone else to lean on will ensure that you can reach above your own potential. You should also seek to be this type of friend to others.

Secondly, it is important to have family. The biology of fathers and mothers is finite, but family is so much more than that. Close friends can be siblings, mentors can be guardians; a family includes those who have invested time and effort into your success. We are supposed to love our family, and in turn, receive love from them. Even if some friends come and go, your family should always stick with you. The bonds and love that tie you and your family together can help you to do your best in everything you face.

Finally, it is important to have God. My faith has shaped so much of what I've accomplished throughout my life. Early on I accepted the fact that we live in an imperfect world: stuff breaks, things hurt, and people die. Even surrounded with a loving family and great friends, this life falls flat. No one will ever be perfect, some of your problems will never be solved, and sometimes you'll not succeed at something. The belief that there is a perfect God and that He loves you, means that you don't have to worry about these things. Every big decision I face, I talk to God about it through prayer. I ask that the right choice is made clear to me, and that I can go forward in confidence. I have found that when I truly rely on God, things always work out for the better. I urge anyone reading this to remember that life isn't meant to be lived alone, but with great friends, a caring family, and a loving God.

BOY SCOUTS OF AMERICA TROOP 1506
EAGLE COURT OF HONOR
FOR
KEVIN LYLE DEVINE
JANUARY 8, 2011

"...those who trust in the Lord will find new strength. They will soar high on wings like eagles..." ~ Isaiah 40:31

Interesting Scouting Facts (from the ceremony in which Kevin was awarded the Rank of Eagle Scout)

For every 100 boys who join Scouting, records indicate that:
- 4 will become Eagle Scouts

A recent nationwide survey of high schools revealed the following information:
- 83% of student council presidents were Scouts

- 89% of senior class presidents were Scouts
- 80% of junior class presidents were Scouts
- 73% of school publication editors were Scouts
- 71% of football captains were Scouts

Scouts also account for:
- 64% of Air Force Academy graduates
- 68% of West Point graduates
- 70% OF ANNAPOLIS GRADUATES
- 72% of Rhodes Scholars
- 85% of F.B.I. agents
- 26 of the first 29 astronauts

* * *

THE ONE DOLLAR BILL *(Take a one dollar bill from your pocket and hold it as you read the following.)*

The one dollar bill you're looking at first came off the presses in its present design in 1957. This so-called "paper" money is in fact a cotton and linen blend, with red and blue minute silk fibers running through it. It is actually fabric material. We've all washed it without its falling apart. A special blend of ink is used, the contents we will never know. It is overprinted with symbols and then it is stretched to make it water resistant and pressed to give it that nice crisp look. If you look on the front of the bill, you will see the United States Treasury Seal. At the top of the Seal you will see the scales for the balance – a balanced budget. In the center you have a carpenter's T-square, a tool used for an even cut. Underneath is the key to the United States Treasury. That's all pretty easy to figure out, but what is on the back of that one dollar bill is something we should all know.

If you turn the bill over, you will see two circles. Both circles, together, comprise the Great Seal of the United

States. The First Continental Congress requested that Benjamin Franklin and a group of men come up with a seal. It took them four years to accomplish this task and another two years to get it approved. If you look at the left-hand circle (the reverse), you will see a pyramid. Notice the face is lighted and the western side is dark. This country was just beginning. We had not begun to explore the West or decide what we could do for Western Civilization. The Pyramid is uncapped, again signifying that we were not even close to being finished. Inside the capstone you have the all-seeing eye, an ancient symbol of divinity.

GREAT SEAL OF THE U.S.   U.S PRESIDENTIAL SEAL

It was Franklin's belief that one man couldn't do it alone, but a group of men, with God, could do anything. "IN GOD WE TRUST" is on this currency. The Latin above the pyramid, ANNUIT CŒPTIS, means "God has favored our undertaking". The Latin below the pyramid, NOVUS ORDO SECLORUM, means "a new order has begun". At the base of the pyramid is a Roman numeral for 1776.

If you look at the right-hand circle (the obverse) on the one dollar bill, and check it carefully, you will see the Great Seal of the United States (above left). You will learn that the Seal is on every National Cemetery in the United

States. It is also on the Parade of Flags Walkway at Bush-nell, Florida National Cemetery, and it is the centerpiece of most heroes' monuments. Slightly modified, it becomes the Seal of the President of the United States (above right) and it is always visible whenever he speaks, yet no one knows what the symbols mean.

The American Bald Eagle was selected as a symbol for victory for two reasons: first, he is not afraid of a storm: he is strong and he is smart enough to soar above it. Secondly, he wears no material crown. We had just broken from the King of England. Across the breast of the Eagle is a shield with 13 alternating red and white stripes (the pales) repre-senting the 13 original States. Also, notice the shield is un-supported. This country now stands on its own. Across the top of the shield is a blue field (chief) that unites all the stripes into one. The blue chief represents the United States Congress. We were coming together as one nation. In the Eagle's beak you will read our first Motto "E PLURIBUS UNUM", meaning "one nation from many people". Above the Eagle you have thirteen stars representing the thirteen original colonies, and any clouds of misunderstanding roll-ing away. Again, we were coming together as one. Notice what the Eagle holds in his talons. He holds an olive branch and a clutch of arrows. This country wants peace, but we will never be afraid to fight to preserve peace. The Eagle always wants to face the olive branch but in time of war, his gaze turns toward the arrows. They say that the number 13 is an unlucky number. This is almost a world-wide belief. Usually, you will never see a room numbered 13, or any hotels or motels with a 13th floor. But think about this: 13 original colonies, 13 signers of the Declaration of Independence, 13 stripes on the U.S. Flag, 13 steps on the pyramid, 13 letters in the Latin above the pyramid, 13 letters in "E Pluribus Unum", 13 stars above the Eagle, 13 plumes of feathers on each span of the Eagle's wings, 13 bars on that shield, 13 leaves on the olive branch, 13 fruits (olives), and if you look closely, 13 arrows. And for minorities: the 13th amendment.

Why don't you know this? Your children don't know this and their history teachers don't know this. Too many veterans have given up too much to ever let the meanings fade. Many veterans remember coming home to an America that didn't care. Too many military men never came home at all. Tell everyone what is on the back of the one dollar bill and what it stands for, because nobody else will.

* * *

The Flag of the United States (aka "The American Flag")

With all the wars the United States has been in, you would think it would be common knowledge of how to display the Flag properly. (Refer to UNITED STATES CODE, Title 36, Chapter 10, Patriotic Customs, Sections 171-177, and UNITED STATES CODE, Title 18, Chapter 33)

How many times have I seen the Flag hanging on a wall backwards: in a bank, in a large hall, at a county fair, in restaurants, and in businesses? The Flag should always be hung with the stars to the left as you face the Flag. At all meetings, in homes, churches, or other places, the Flag of the United States of America should always be placed to the right of the presiding officer or speaker.

I recall one occasion that was particularly and exceptionally embarrassing. It was a National Holiday and many veterans were in attendance at the program provided for the occasion. The Flag was hung backwards and nobody noticed.

Incidentally, the Pledge of Allegiance to the Flag is:

"I pledge allegiance to the Flag of the United States of America, and to the Republic for which it stands, one Nation under God, indivisible, with liberty and justice for all."

It should be rendered by standing at attention facing the Flag with the right hand over the heart. Persons in uniform should remain silent, face the Flag, and render the military salute.

MEANING OF THE FLAG DRAPED COFFIN

Have you ever noticed how an Honour Guard pays meticulous attention to correctly folding the United States of America Flag 13 times? You probably thought it was to symbolize the original 13 colonies, but we learn something new every day!

The flag-folding ceremony represents the same religious principles on which our great country was originally founded.

The portion of the flag denoting honor is the canton of blue containing the stars representing states our veterans served in uniform. The canton field of blue dresses from left to right and is inverted only when draped as a pall on the casket of a veteran who has served our country honorably in uniform.

In the U.S. Armed Forces, at the ceremony of retreat, the flag is lowered, folded in a triangle fold and kept under watch throughout the night as a tribute to our nation's honored dead. The next morning it is brought out and, at the ceremony of reveille, run aloft as a symbol of our belief in the resurrection of the body.

The source and the date of origin of this Flag Folding Procedure is unknown, however some sources attribute it to the Gold Star Mothers of America while others to an Air Force Chaplain stationed at the United States Air Force Academy. Others consider it to be an urban legend. It is provided as a patriotic service to all.

The traditional method of folding
the flag is as follows:

(A) Straighten out the flag to full length and fold lengthwise once.

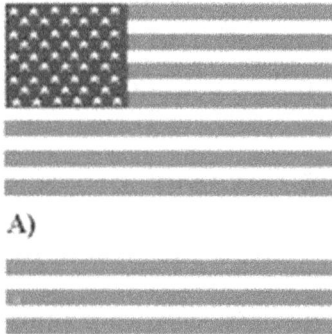

A)

THE **FIRST FOLD** OF OUR FLAG IS A SYMBOL OF LIFE." **(A)**

(B) Fold it lengthwise a second time to meet the open edge, making sure that the union of stars on the blue field remains outward in full view. (A large flag may have to be folded lengthwise a third time.)

B)

"THE **SECOND** FOLD IS A SYMBOL OF OUR BELIEF IN ETER-
NAL LIFE." **(B)**

(C) A triangular fold is then started by bringing the striped corner of the folded edge to the open edge.

C)

"THE **THIRD** FOLD IS MADE IN HONOR AND REMEMBRANCE OF THE VETERAN DEPARTING OUR RANKS, AND WHO GAVE A PORTION OF HIS OR HER LIFE FOR THE DEFENSE OF OUR COUN-TRY TO ATTAIN PEACE THROUGHOUT THE WORLD." **(C)**

(D) The outer point is then turned inward, parallel with the open edge, to form a second triangle.

D)

"THE **FOURTH** FOLD REPRESENTS OUR WEAKER NATURE; AS AMERICAN CITIZENS TRUSTING IN GOD, IT IS TO HIM WE TURN IN TIMES OF PEACE, AS WELL AS IN TIMES OF WAR, FOR HIS DI-VINE GUIDANCE." **(D)**

(E) The diagonal or triangular folding is continued toward the blue union until the end is reached, with only the blue showing and the form being that of a cocked (three-corner) hat.

E)

"THE **FIFTH FOLD** IS A TRIBUTE TO OUR COUNTRY, FOR IN THE WORDS OF STEPHEN DECATUR, 'OUR COUNTRY, IN DEALING WITH OTHER COUNTRIES, MAY SHE ALWAYS BE RIGHT, BUT IT IS STILL OUR COUNTRY, RIGHT OR WRONG'." **(E)**

"THE **SIXTH FOLD** IS FOR WHERE OUR HEARTS LIE. IT IS WITH OUR HEART THAT WE PLEDGE ALLEGIANCE TO THE FLAG OF THE UNITED STATES OF AMERICA, AND TO THE REPUBLIC FOR WHICH IT STANDS, ONE NATION UNDER GOD, INDIVISIBLE, WITH LIBERTY AND JUSTICE FOR ALL." **(E)**

"THE **SEVENTH FOLD** IS A TRIBUTE TO OUR ARMED FORCES, FOR IT IS THROUGH THE ARMED FORCES THAT WE PROTECT OUR COUNTRY AND OUR FLAG AGAINST ALL ENEMIES, WHETHER THEY BE FOUND WITHIN OR WITHOUT THE BOUNDARIES OF OUR REPUBLIC." **(E)**

"THE **EIGHTH FOLD** IS A TRIBUTE TO THE ONE WHO ENTERED INTO THE VALLEY OF THE SHADOW OF DEATH, THAT WE MIGHT SEE THE LIGHT OF DAY, AND TO HONOR OUR MOTHERS, FOR WHOM IT FLIES ON MOTHER'S DAY." **(E)**

"THE **NINTH FOLD** IS A TRIBUTE TO WOMANHOOD, FOR IT HAS BEEN THROUGH THEIR FAITH, LOVE, LOYALTY AND DEVOTION THAT THE CHARACTERS OF THE MEN AND WOMEN WHO HAVE MADE THIS COUNTRY GREAT HAVE BEEN MOLDED." **(E)**

"THE **10TH FOLD** IS A TRIBUTE TO THE FATHER, FOR HE, TOO, HAS GIVEN HIS SONS AND DAUGHTERS FOR THE DEFENSE OF OUR COUNTRY SINCE HE OR SHE WAS FIRST BORN." **(E)**

"THE **11TH FOLD**, IN THE EYES OF HEBREW CITIZENS, REPRESENTS THE LOWER PORTION OF THE SEAL OF KING DAVID AND KING SOLOMON AND GLORIFIES, IN THEIR EYES, THE GOD OF ABRAHAM, ISAAC AND JACOB." **(E)**

"THE **12TH FOLD**, IN THE EYES OF A CHRISTIAN CITIZEN, REPRESENTS AN EMBLEM OF ETERNITY AND GLORIFIES, IN THEIR EYES, GOD THE FATHER, THE SON AND HOLY GHOST." **(E)**

"ON THE **13TH FOLD**, OR WHEN THE FLAG IS COMPLETELY FOLDED, THE STARS ARE UPPERMOST, REMINDING US OF OUR NATIONAL MOTTO, 'IN GOD WE TRUST'." **(E)**

After the flag is completely folded and tucked in, it has the appearance of a cocked hat, ever reminding us of the soldiers who served under Gen. George Washington and the sailors and Marines who served under Capt. John Paul Jones and were followed by their comrades and shipmates in the U.S. Armed Forces, preserving for us the rights, privileges and freedoms we enjoy today.

HOW A BILL BECOMES A LAW

About 25,000 bills are introduced in each term of Congress, but only 10% become law. The following are the steps in the law-making process. A bill may begin in either the House or the Senate except for money bills, which must be introduced in the House.

1. A Bill is Drafted: Members of Congress, the Executive Branch, and outside groups can draft (write or draw up) bills.

2. The Bill is Introduced in House: Representative introduces the bill in the House. Only members can introduce bills.

3. Sent to Committee: The Speaker of the House sends the bill to the appropriate standing committee. The committee chair then assigns the bill to a subcommittee, which holds hearings. After consideration of the results of those hearings, the subcommittee votes on the bill and any proposed amendments. If passed, the bill is sent to the full committee.

4. Committee Action: Most bills die here. The committee may pigeonhole, table, amend, or vote on the bill. If the bill passes, it goes to the Rules Committee.

5. Rules Committee (Only in the House): It decides the rules for debate, and when the bill will come up for debate. The "rules" given a bill can have a major impact on its chances of passing.

6. Floor Action: House debates the bill, and may add amendments. If a majority votes in favor of the bill, it goes to the Senate.

7. Introduced in Senate: A Senator introduces the bill, which is sent to a committee.

8. Committee Action: Same procedure as in the House. If the committee majority votes for the bill, it goes to the whole Senate.

9. The Bill is Called Up: The Senate Majority Floor Leader decides when the whole Senate will consider the bill.

10. Floor Action: The Bill is debated, and amendments may be added. If a majority votes in favor of the bill, it is returned to the House.

11. Conference Committee: If the House rejects any of the changes (made by the Senate), the bill goes to a conference committee of members from both houses. It works out a compromise.

12. Vote on Compromise: Both houses must approve changes made by the conference committee. If approved, the bill goes to the President.

13. Presidential Action: The President may sign (approve) the bill or veto (reject) it. If the President takes no action within ten days, the bill becomes law.

14. Vote to Override: If the President vetoes the bill, it returns to Congress for another vote. If two-thirds of the members of both house vote for the bill, it becomes law over the President's veto. If either House falls short of a two-thirds majority, the bill is defeated.

In Practice, the process remains the same, but politicians often earn their reputations by the ploys they use while making laws.

These strategies include: "log-rolling", in which two or more representatives "trade" votes to effectively promote their individual and special interests in bills that may not be remotely similar; and "pork-barreling", a group activity closely related to log-rolling. It represents an investment of public monies in something that is not necessary, just to keep jobs and federal funds in the state. A senator participating in this ploy may be seen by his constituents as "bringing home the bacon".

Members of Congress do not spend all of their time engaged in law-making and governing. In fact, they spend an enormous amount of time making sure that they will be re-elected.

One of the most powerful tools they can use is the **FRANKING PRIVILEGE**: Members of Congress are not charged postage fees to send mail to constituents in their district or state.

Another special tool that greatly advantages members of Congress in their re-election bids is their STAFF, which may number upwards of twenty people. They provide a public relations advantage at election time by helping cut through the red tape.

Finally, as members of Congress, incumbents are in great demand for speaking engagements, to appear in parades, at barbecues, ground-breakings, and other public ceremonies with HIGH PROFILE EXPOSURE (aka Photo Opportunities).

The reality of practical politics requires that "WE THE PEOPLE..." exercise careful oversight and maintenance of those Representatives and Senators that We (the People) have elected to Congress. As responsible citizens, we MUST monitor our elected officials to make sure they are representing OUR best interests.

The following are some easy ways to find out what your representatives are doing:

1. Start with something basic. What committees and sub-committees have they been assigned to? Do they hold a position of seniority on any committee? The chair of a House or Senate committee can wield a great deal of power.

2. Another easy area to track is voting participation scores. Simply put, how often did they vote last year? The year before? How often did they vote with the President's position? With members of their own party? If they are frequently not present to vote, then they are not doing the job to which they were elected.

3. Compare their campaign promises to their actual performance once in office. As an example, what about the issue of abortion. Did they support or oppose abortion counseling at federal clinics? How does their position compare with yours?

4. Check their campaign finance history for their last full cycle. Look at the committees they serve on and then see if they take any PACs (Political Action Committees) donations. Where is their funding coming from?

5. Check frequently to see how your representatives are voting on issues that are important to you. They are not likely to report to you each time they vote on a health care issue, so it is up to you to check and find out.

REMEMBER: You are their employer! You have a right and a civic obligation to communicate with your representatives. You should be doing the "first and foremost" influencing – **NOT** the lobbyists.

JURY DUTY

Have you ever been called to serve on a jury? To actually serve on a jury is every person's personal responsibility, at least once in their lifetime. Life has not completed a full circle until you have done this. I have been called several times in my mid-years, but my union has always gotten me excused. Later, after retirement, I have been called but the cases were settled without court action. At the age of eighty-seven, I was called and did get to serve. It was a true satisfaction at first, but soon became a very serious situation. It taxes the very deepest part of your soul and your mental capacity to come to the right decision. This is what made jury duty for me such a satisfaction – to accept this responsibility to society. If you don't have the guts to do this, maybe you would feel better moving to a country where you could have more freedom and less responsibility. In serving on jury, I met people from several walks of life and they were so interesting, knowledgeable, and kind. It was an experience I will treasure the rest of my life.

Chapter Five

The Disaster Years

One of the shocking times in the Tunnel of Life is the disaster years. You discover that up ahead the tunnel separates (you know why). It often had unexpected turns and dips, and was sometimes difficult to manage, but now you realize you are not ready for this day of reckoning. You have often wondered about this time in life. It becomes evident that you might not know how to cope with it when it arrives. You think, am I going to be a piker and pass on first leaving my spouse to do all the suffering, or how will I survive being the last to finish the tunnel of life alone? The problem is, the longer you live life together, the worse the pain. The solution: Just think of the unlucky ones who lose faith in one another, and face the tunnel of life alone. There is no love to shore them up when life is almost over.

There is nothing but emptiness if you don't have faith. The ones who reach this point with love and a faithful spouse have the easiest route. When it comes to old age and you start assessing your situation and all the sacred things you accumulated over the years, what do you do with them now?

They don't seem to hold the same value they once did for you. Your needs have changed drastically, but some possessions do hold sentimental or real value. More than anything, it's the hurt you experience in getting rid of them. It means your life has less meaning than it once held, you feel so alone, and it's a loneliness you have never felt before. Part of it is having your friends and family slowly dwindle in size. Life in general has less meaning and it's actually closing in on you. For the most part, you live in reminiscences and have to be satisfied. When you reach this point in life, your mind occasionally drifts to thoughts such as: How much time do you have left on this earth? How long will your spouse live? Is your financial capacity sufficient to carry you through to the end in some semblance of comfort? Memory has a life of its own. One thing I've noticed on different occasions is that when you don't remember what actually happened and how you handled a situation, years later in conversation with your children or others, you discover that it could have been handled better or differently. The final analysis, however, is the love and respect or lack of it that comes from those who know you best. Your life is only as successful as others who know you, see you. This has nothing to do with your religious calm and peace of mind; from that standpoint, your moral satisfaction has been a part of you all your life, in one way or another, and you build on it as you lived your life.

When you are leaving the Golden Years and entering the Disaster years, hopefully you still have some semblance of what is going on. You find each day is easier, because all of life's challenges, even the ones you did in the Golden Years because you wanted to, are gone. You can just relax and let the day do its thing or nothing at all. At any rate, old age and the tunnel of life have a plan of their own and you are just a follower. You cannot do anything about it. If you do not have pain someplace, then life is enjoyable. This is the time when Father Time takes over and your golden faculties are diminished to little or nothing. The only comfort you have mentally comes from whatever remembrances you have that merit acknowledgment and your faith in God. Whatever desires you had in life, if you didn't do them when you had the chance, you have to live with that. There is no going back – the tunnel of life goes in one direction only.

The Disaster years encompass the short time in life after your Golden Years. This is a time in your life when you take poll of where you are in all phases of life. To expand on this, you need to analyze the time you probably have left on this earth, and make the most of it – to clean up loose ends, to find that peace of mind you deserve and to take care of those people left behind that you feel responsible for in whatever way you can. This time may be only a short time and very unpredictable, but if it expands into a very long time, it truly becomes the disaster years. This time comes when you want to go from here to over there and it requires that you step up; the feet say "STEP UP", but the knees say "NO WAY, WE CAN'T DO THAT ANYMORE." You start to write something down, but the hand doesn't obey what your mind is telling it to do. At the worst, you may decide to go to Wisconsin (no reason, it just sounds like fun), you go outside, start walking, get lost (disoriented), and someone has to go find you. During this time, a cane or a walker is your best friend, and you spend more time in bed than not. Your heart says it can't handle the stress, you don't get the oxygen needed for the body to function properly, you're tired all the time, and day and night may get confusing. You have two factors to put up with: the body and the mind. If the mind goes first, the body can't function; but if the body goes first, the mind can express pleasure or anger, it can reminisce, and you may go out with some semblance of dignity. This is a time when all the things you took for granted are no more, like walking over uneven ground. The greatest disservice to older people is the lack of comprehension or understanding by the younger set when you say "I CAN'T DO IT." This is beyond "I'M AFRAID TO DO IT." This is a time when physical therapy is not the answer. There really is NO answer. To those who experience the far end of the tunnel of life where disease, drugs, or body functions just wear out, bedridden, and striving for that last breath of air and death; it would seem morally logical to at some point before all this happens, you would gather loved ones, family, and friends around to have closure while you can, and then take care of the pain with insentient death.

Yesterday I read in the newspaper about an organization called "Now I lay me down to sleep". What they are doing is to go to families all over the country who have babies dying, and they take professional photos of the baby for the family. This gives solace and remembrance to the families of each beloved baby. It reminded me that the same thing happened in my own life, because the opportunity was there. I had some neighbors, a couple whom I got to know quite well when my wife and I lived in leisure town. He had been a well-respected lawyer in his day and his wife held a high position at Kaiser Permanente. She had cancer, didn't have much time left, and had come home from the hospital to die. I had an old trusty Clarus camera (now about sixty years old) with a portrait lens. I walked across the street and made arrangements with the man to take portrait pictures of each of them, so they would always have the latest remembrance of each other for all time. He said yes, so I had him stand in an exact spot in front of his house for his picture; then he helped his wife come out and I took her picture the same way. Thank God the pictures come out perfectly, and I gave them a 9x12 picture of each other. The next day they came across the street and sat on our couch visiting for a few minutes. I am sure we were the last outing she had, but they could, at least for those last days, sit and enjoy their familiar surroundings and be happy together. There isn't much time between pains in which a person can savor happiness, and you have to take these precious moments when you can get them. I didn't realize when I took those pictures, just how much life was breathed into that couple's lives. That was five years ago, she passed on, and he is in a home now and doesn't really know what is going on, but I am sure for about four years he got enjoyment and happiness looking at his wife's last picture.

The Tunnel of Life

* * *

This story of unconscionable result really belongs in the Disaster Years. This should never happen to anyone, but all too often it does. I don't like using examples from my own life because I wanted this book to be about other peoples' lives. Unfortunately, this story needs to be told. It should have been a wake-up call for all of us because, at the time, my older brother was at a point where he could hardly walk from his house to his car without having to rest before getting into it. My younger brother was trying to get him to go into assisted living, but like most people, he didn't like accepting this fact of life. He finally realized that it was for the best. However, it seemed like he was in the hospital as much as in assisted living. Our family was about to have a reunion in South Dakota, but when it came time for the reunion, he was in the hospital and could not go. Before the reunion, the family at home went to see him and visit around. At this time he was sitting up in a chair beside his bed at the hospital. He seemed at ease and was visiting with everyone who came. We were told that he was retaining fluid, so they were giving him large doses of medication. They were also concerned about his blood pressure, and he had been given kidney dialysis. They found large amounts of protein and calcium in his blood. My younger brother later told me that our brother had asked him "Is this the way it's going to be? I hurt all over." He was grasping for answers and not getting them. This is when we could have had some meaningful goodbyes with him, while everyone was there, just before the reunion. We didn't know his time was that short.

After the reunion in South Dakota, we all went our separate ways home. When I got home to California, I called my son Brian, an X-ray technician. Having worked alongside many doctors for years, Brian knew right away what was happening. My son said that if my brother had high amounts of protein and calcium in his blood, his body systems were shutting down and he could die at any time, or he could last a short time. This is when I decided to return to Minnesota and be with my brother. I drove because I didn't know how long I would be gone. Only one day into the trip, my younger brother called me. Our brother had died.

Now, if my son (the x-ray technician) knew the possible situation, why did the doctors not give us some kind of warning or heads-up a week earlier when we were all there? We could have said goodbye to him properly instead of expressing nothing. I don't understand this, and it has nothing to do with the doctors' fears of reprisal.

I AM A SICK AMERICAN

There are those who claim ours is a "sick"' society; that our country is sick: that we are sick. Well, maybe they're right, I submit that I'm sick. . .and maybe you are, too. I am sick of having policemen ridiculed and called "pigs" while cop killers are hailed as some kind of folk hero.

I AM SICK of being told that religion is the opiate of the people, but marijuana should be legalized.

I AM SICK of commentators and columnists canonizing anarchists, revolutionaries and criminal rapists, but condemning law enforcement when such criminals are brought to justice.

I AM SICK of being told that pornography is the right of the free press, but freedom of the press does not include being able to read the Bible on school grounds.

I AM SICK of paying more and more taxes to build schools while I see some faculty members encouraging students either to tear them down or burn them.

I AM SICK of Supreme Court decisions which turn criminals loose on society while other decisions try to take away my means of protecting my home and family.

I AM SICK of pot-smoking entertainers deluging me with their condemnation of my moral standards on late-night television.

I AM SICK of being told that policemen are mad dogs who should not have guns, but that criminals who use guns to rob, maim and murder should be understood and helped back to society.

I AM SICK of being told it is wrong to use napalm to end a war overseas but if it's a Molotov cocktail or a bomb at home, I must understand the provocations.

I AM SICK of not being able to take my family to a movie unless I want to have them exposed to nudity, homosexuality and the glorification of narcotics.

I AM SICK of riots, marches, protests, demonstrations, confrontations, and the other mob temper tantrums of people intellectually incapable of working within the system.

I AM SICK of hearing the same slick slogans, the cries of people who must chant the same thing like zombies because they haven't the capacity for verbalizing thought.

I AM SICK of those who say I owe them this or that because of the sins of my forefathers when I have looked down both ends of a gun barrel to defend their rights, their liberties and their families.

I AM SICK of cynical attitudes toward patriotism. I am sick of politicians with no backbone.

I AM SICK of permissiveness.

I AM SICK of the dirty, the foulmouthed, the unwashed.

I AM SICK of the decline of personal honesty, personal integrity and human sincerity.

Most of all, though, I AM SICK of being told I'm sick.

I AM SICK of being told my country is sick — when we have the greatest nation that man has ever brought forth on the face of the earth. Fully 50% of the people on earth would willingly trade places with the most deprived, the most underprivileged among us. Yes, I may be sick, but if I am only sick, I can get well. I can also help my society get well and help my country get well.

Take note, all of you . . . you will not find me throwing a rock or a bomb; you will not find me under a placard; you will not see me take to the streets; you will not find me ranting to wild-eyed mobs.

But you will find me at work, paying taxes, serving in the community where I live. You will also find me expressing my anger and indignation to elected officials.

You will find me speaking out in support of those officials, institutions and personalities who contribute to the elevation of society and not its destruction. You will find me contributing my time, money and personal influence to helping churches, hospitals, charities and other establishments which have shown the true spirit of this country's determination to ease pain, suffering, eliminate hunger, and generate brotherhood.

But, most of all, you'll find me at the polling place. There — if you listen — you can hear the thunder of the common man. There, all of us can cast our vote—for an America where people can walk the streets without fear. ~AUTHOR UNKNOWN

JAKE

This is the story about the life of a particular machinist who did only PROTOTYPE works. That means he created one- or two-of-a-kind experimental parts that would be tested to see if they worked or performed successfully before they were put into production.

Jake got his training in the Navy, and apparently the Navy training was the very best because his life consisted of always doing the impossible. Most of his jobs were things no one else would touch, or if they did, the tolerances allowed didn't hold or the part (prototype) they created developed problems of one kind or another before it was completed.

For the most part, Jake did work for the space industry or commercial industry. What a machinist does first is look at a part that the engineering department has come up with. The machinist decides how to hold onto the material of which the part will be made and what procedures must be done first, second, third, and so on to the part so it can be held in a lathe or mill to perform each process. Also the machinist is the last person to challenge all radiuses, bores, finishes, depths and angles so some hole doesn't come clear through where it isn't supposed to.

If possible, the machinist has to reason if the part is feasible before he sends it back to engineering for approval.

This ability only comes with experience. There can be no mistakes on flight or space equipment. There is so much to lose if failure cannot be discovered before anything is accepted and performance is accurate

Machinists are in great demand and you might even say they are a dying breed. Accuracy is the final and only word accepted in this trade. Just like a skilled surgeon or master electrician, they know the outcome before they start.

Jake and all those engineers have created tons of individual pieces of equipment that float around in space, on commercial airlines and in other inventions, performing the tasks for which they were designed and machined with "accuracy".

This country was founded, in my opinion, on a few highly respected, intelligent, sincere, and politically aware people and a very dedicated military. Since then, and because of them, we have advanced in many ways.

We should be eternally grateful for all our engineers, machinists, military service people, doctors, electricians, electronic geniuses and everyone else who keep this country on an even keel. It all comes from education, principles, and dedication to the higher good.

In 2014, the United States lost one of the finest space engineers we've ever had – Clayton D. Bushnell. I wonder if there will ever be another one like him.

LBD TO LYLE

This retired soldier has been in several countries during his numerous tours of duty, including Germany, Korea, Turkey, Iraq, and Kuwait. The unusual thing about him is that he had his mind made up when he was in high school as to what he would become. Keep in mind that he had to cope with extreme dyslexia from his beginnings, so here is his story.

I guess I will write about the most dominant part of my life. When I was in Junior High School I set goals for myself. That was something kids today don't know anything about. My first goal was to join the Army and earn a retirement; second was to build a house, and third was to have a goal I could never accomplish so I would have something to strive for. (Author Note: I left out the specifics of his third goal because it isn't relative at this point, but it was needed for a goal. It was a pretty hair-raising challenge.)

After High School, I joined the Army and volunteered for a tour in Turkey. I found out that was a big mistake. Here were 25 guys in the middle of the desert with a very boring job; for entertainment we would go out shooting wild dogs. It was fun, but kind of dangerous; these dogs were mean and ran in packs. If you were on "C Q" (charge of quarters), at midnight – 0001 to be exact – the green box, which is the phone, would ring and there would be a female on the other end of the line. That was a big thrill to hear her voice.

After that tour, I was sent to Fort Lewis, Washington, where I was in field artillery. You learn many things in the military. I met my first wife there. Her name was Lucinda and we had two children – Loren (the 2nd) and Kimberly. From there we went to Fort Sill, Oklahoma. After this tour, I was transferred overseas to Germany. I liked my time there. My next base was Fort Campbell, Kentucky. While I was overseas in Germany, my wife met someone else, so we got divorced. She still lives with her husband Todd and my kids in Michigan. I then went back to Nuremburg, Germany for another tour. The divorce papers followed me there. I got out of the field artillery and started driving semi-trucks.

When I came back to the states I took a break from the military and took a job with a small building contractor (general contractor). He built mostly large deluxe homes, one at a time. So I did get to build a house as I had planned. I had been married for the second time to Kim for a short time, and had volunteered for Desert Storm. She was mad at me for a little while for that, but she and I had known each other for years – we were best friends in High School. Because she knew how I was, she supported my decision. I arrived in Baghdad and had a new "mess" thrown at me. This was a new job of salvaging and collecting enemy weaponry in Desert Storm. My job was to go in after a place was bombed and take Grave Administration along with me. I would salvage all the munitions while Grave Administration would pick up all the bodies or parts and tag them. It was not a fun job. One time I was to pick up two of our tanks that were strafed and hit by our own planes – this mission never happened, so to speak. It wasn't ever talked about. I still have nightmares about climbing into those tanks and seeing nothing of the four soldiers inside. I had to clear the tanks of munitions so we could transfer them safely...God, I never talked about that for years. I've tried to forget, but it still haunts me. One time we were going to a pick up when the road was bombed. There were body parts everywhere. You can't explain to anybody how it feels or smells. I can't talk about this, it makes me depressed. When I came home from Desert Storm I had two good friends: Chief Gill and a guy we called the GRAVE ROBBER. He was in the Grave Administration; I never knew his real name. Chief Gill died of cancer a few years later, and the GRAVE ROBBER couldn't take it anymore and shot himself. I had a tattoo put on my arm of a "3" to remember them. Kim and I have two great kids, Shawn and

Kaitlin. I retired from the Army and we live in Las Vegas now. This was my last tour station. I still try to cope with my demons. My shrink helps but in the end it's still all on my shoulders. It's just one of those things you have to live with and I keep telling myself everything will be okay. I hope so!!!

HELEN BRINKS, PAMELA KIMPSON, AND GARY BRINKS – RELAY FOR LIFE

I imagine all of you know by now that Gary will not be with us at the Relay tonight. This morning he had surgery at Sioux Valley Hospital to repair what the doctor called a huge herniated disk that was pressing on his sciatic nerve. I am happy to report that the acute pain that has been in his back and leg is gone. He is looking forward to sitting and standing again without terrible pain.

I would like to thank everyone for their concern and prayers this last week while we have been doctoring. Thank you to those of you at work who covered for me so I could be with Gary. We are so very, very thankful that it was only a disc and not a cancerous tumor pressing on the nerve. Whenever Gary has a new health problem we always worry about cancer – just like you cancer survivors. Whenever you have a new ache or pain, or a new symptom, there is always the fear of cancer. It is a very real fear that you live with each day, and it is a fear we must control and not let it control us.

I have just gotten back from the hospital and Gary wanted me to be sure and greet you, thank you, and wish you well on another successful year. He hopes the weather will cooperate tonight. He really feels bad having to miss the activities tonight – I wish that there was closed circuit TV so he could watch the Relay over there. He wants you to remember that even though he isn't here tonight he will be here in thoughts and prayers. I would also like to thank our daughter Pamela for agreeing to stand in for her Dad tonight. *Helen*

My name is Pamela Kimpson and I am here representing my Dad. For those of you that know my Dad, you know when he says he will do something for you he will do it no matter what, so this is really hard on him not being able to be up here and talk to you tonight. We are thankful he had the back surgery to relieve the pain in his back and legs. I am very proud of my Dad and how he has handled all the trials and tribulations that have come his way the last three years. He is an example to us all in keeping the Faith. I would like to introduce my family. My Mom Helen works at the Regional Development Commission, and both Mom and Dad are on the Center for Regional Development Team; my brother Aaron is on the Murray County 4-H Ambassador Team; my sister Sara is helping with the FLA Team, and my sister Laura was unable to be here tonight. Dad is very honored to have their support and to know they've been through a lot too in the past 3-1/2 years. At this time I would like to share the thoughts that Dad had prepared for tonight's Relay For Life.

My name is Gary Brinks and I am a cancer survivor. I was diagnosed with Non-Hodgkins Lymphoma in January of 1997. A few years before, this type and other kinds of cancer would have meant a death sentence; but thanks to cancer research, new strides have been made in the treatment and cure of many cancers. This research is made possible by events such as this Relay that we are having tonight. Many of you are familiar with my story, but for those of you who are not, I will quickly re-cap 1997.

During December, 1996, I noticed tightness in my throat area while I was assessing. We had a vacation planned for December 26th to January 6th, so I was trying to do as much assessing as I could in between snow storms and ice storms. Part of the reason for going was my daughter and her fiancée wanted to look *at a seminary in Pasadena, California. Before we left, I went to the doctor because of this tightness in my throat. He said to go to California, but scheduled me for thyroid tests when I got back in January. During our stay in California, my throat only got worse and on January 3rd I went to an Emergency Room in California and the doctor there advised getting home as soon as we could. The pressure in my head was so great I could hardly stand it – flying was out of the question with the changes in altitude. We drove straight home in 30 hours between snowstorms. The Lord was really looking out for us because Interstate I-29 had just opened up before we got to Omaha to head north to Sioux Falls.*

I entered Sioux Valley Hospital on January 6th – they began immediately to schedule x-rays, blood tests, and CAT scans. That night they tried to do a biopsy guided by a CAT scan, but they couldn't get enough cells to test. The tumor in my chest cavity was growing so fast it was cutting off my breathing so they admitted me into Intensive Care and put me on a ventilator. The next day they did surgery and the biopsy confirmed the diagnosis of Non-Hodgkins Lymphoma. The chemo didn't seem to be working fast enough so they started full chest radiation in an attempt to slow the cancer. This resulted in burning my chest, back, and throat so badly I could hardly eat or drink and I lost about 60 pounds. I had 20 radiation treatments and had a regimen of chemo every three weeks. It was called a super CHOP chemo and I found out later this dosage plus the radiation was all my body could handle.

Ten days after each chemo treatment, I would have to go to the hospital and get shots to build up my blood. A week or so after each treatment I would get so dehydrated I would have to go to the hospital for a few days of IVs. All together I spend over 60 days in the hospital in 1997.

I then developed PCP pneumonia in April so they stopped the chemo treatments for a couple of months. In spite of the PCP pneumonia which they treated with IVs for four weeks, I was able to attend my daughter's college graduation and a month later I walked her down the aisle at her wedding.

After the wedding the doctors resumed the chemo treatments until I developed a shoulder infection which required two surgeries and more outpatient IVs.

You might say that cancer saved my life. Because of the initial Non-Hodgkins Lymphoma, I had abdominal scans that revealed a cancerous kidney. Most times by the time there are symptoms with kidney cancer, it is too late. In September, after my chemo was done they did an evaluation and decided to remove my kidney in late October when I was stronger. I was fortunate that it was all contained – yet another miracle in my life. They also discovered that I had a spot on my back that was melanoma so they removed that and it was also contained. These were three independent kinds of cancer.

I would like to thank the community again for all of their support – I couldn't have made it through these past 3 years without all of the help of family, friends, and the community. Each day that goes by I realize people are still supporting and praying for us. I also know my family suffered as much as I did only in a different way. My wife Helen balanced working outside the home, taking care of me, and making trips to doctor appointments as well as trying to keep home life normal for our son Aaron, who was 15, and our daughter Sara, who was 11. Our two older girls Laura and Pamela visited often but it was harder on the kids at home because they saw me get weaker each day. Initially, I didn't think much about what I had; I wasn't scared and somehow I knew I would be all right. It seemed like everybody all over the country was praying for me and I knew the Lord would answer our prayers. After many more times in the hospital and other complications, I developed different feelings – like I don't care anymore, that the Lord should take me because I knew I was putting my family through such difficult times. In November, after my kidney surgery, when things seemed to be getting better, my Dad died. My Dad had helped me farm for over 20 years and this was just another blow. I didn't realize it at the time, but a few months later I was diagnosed with severe depression which quite often happens after major trauma and surgery. I am being treated for that with medications which have kept it under control. The last couple of years have been a healing process that seems like it takes forever, but I am feeling better all the time and am almost back to normal. I will always have to take medications, most of which are because of the cancer treatment, not the cancers. Also, very humid days make it hard to breathe because the radiation was very hard on my lungs. My immune system is poor so I have to watch out for infection. Also chemo has weakened my bones so that is why I'm having back and spine problems now and will have to have surgery.

Cancer is a terrible word to hear or say, but I can truthfully say it has changed my life completely for the good, even if problems keep arising. Every day to me is a gift from God and I pray each day that I make the most of each day because life is so short. Do things with your friends and family – these are the things that they will never forget. If you are working all the time and don't take the time, there will be no memories. Let God be first in your life – if you know the Lord, you know where you will spend eternal life. This gives you the strength and the hope you need to get through the difficult times in life. Be thankful for what you have – I know we all want more things, but we are so blessed already in what we have. The Lord does provide what you really need in life. Remember that cancer can be cured and stopped.

Every day more cures and treatments are being discovered. It is Relay For Life and other fund raisers like this that provide the researchers with the funds to find these new cures and treatments. I am so thankful to all of you who support the Relay For Life and are here to show that you care. At some point in our lives we will all be affected by cancer, either directly or indirectly by someone we love. Don't give up hope – more and more people are surviving each year and better treatments are being developed so that the treatments aren't as hard on a person.

I know that all of you that come tonight or have helped and supported this even care. Caring and loving are the things we can do for each other every minute of each day. Praying for each other is another thing we can do – Praying gives us Hope. That's the one thing through my treatments and afterwards that I'll never forget. You don't know what it means to have somebody say they are praying for you or will pray with you. Our prayers are always answered – maybe not the way we would want, but the Lord will always take care of us.

I would like to close with a poem from the book **Chicken Soup for the Surviving Soul** *entitled:*

"Surviving Cancer"
It seems like only yesterday
My doctor told me I had cancer
And when I asked, "how long do I have?"
He didn't have an answer.

And it seems to me that time stood still
And the room turned upside down.

The Tunnel of Life

Life just stopped and stared at him
And I didn't hear a sound.

And a thousand years flashed by my eyes
As I thought of all I'd miss,
Of the laughs and smiles of those I loved
And my two-year old daughter's kiss.

And I realized right then and there
The time that I had wasted,
Of all the things I'd never done
And all the life untasted.

And I thought of all the silly things
That occupied our day,
Like the stupid fight we had last night
Over bills we had to pay.

And I'm still at the dance.
Twenty years have come and gone
I guess that God just changed His mind
And gave me another chance.

And on that day I took a vow
To let go of the past,
To live my life and love each day
As if it were my last.

For only God can know these things
The day, the hour, the time,
But on this day I am alive

And all the world is mine.

My message tonight has been one of hope and that is what Relays are all about. I would like to thank the committee for asking me to be the honorary chairperson of the Year 2000 Relay for Life. I would like to thank all of you again for your support for this wonderful fundraiser for cancer research. Thank you. Gary.

HELEN BRINKS, SLAYTON MN

FAITH – FAMILY – FRIENDS

I can't begin to tell you how important the 3 "Fs" have become in my life in 2014. In January, I turned 65 and anticipated finishing my last year of employment as Financial Support for the South Regional Development Commission of Southwest Minnesota (my employer for the past 30 years). My 65th birthday was uneventful until I had my yearly mammogram and got that dreaded phone call that something didn't seem quite right, that I needed to have a second one done, and to make an appointment with another doctor. Much to my surprise, a positive biopsy result was just the beginning of many emotions that would flood my next 12 months. Things moved very quickly and I found myself going through this cancer journey with 30 daily radiation treatments to a town 30 miles away thinking "I am so glad I have my Faith, Family and Friends to support me in this journey. It was hard to really wrap my brain around what was actually going on as it all happened so fast. When I think back to the months of January through April it is kind of a blur as I was so busy running to doctor appointments and radiation treatments and trying to fit in my 40 hours of work each week and not miss a beat with my family, which included my husband and 4 children and their families. I must admit I maybe did push my-

self a bit much to make it all work, but I was bound and determined this was not going to get me down and I was going to come out on top of this cancer. I had been on this journey with my husband 17 years before and I saw the toll it took on our family then and I was determined that my cancer was not going to do that again to our family. I had grandchildren to be involved with and a church family as well as my husband to show that Cancer can't stop me and just how strong I really was. Of course I was not about to miss any work either; I was going to show them and myself just how tough I really was.

My husband and I are very active participants in the Relay For Life of Murray County. I must admit the Relay has always been very meaningful for me, but this year being my first year as a survivor was beyond words. The emotions overcame me that evening in August as I walked in the Survivor Lap with my husband by my side. It is one of those important "F" moments in my life when Faith, Family and Friends were very evident in my life.

My life seemed to be going along at a very rapid pace as my retirement was fast approaching. Gary and I were anticipating the upcoming trip to Mexico with our son's family the end of October, when I was bothered with a cough that just would not go away.

Well, you guessed it...the results were not what I wanted to hear...a very long and frustrating story told short...they found lung cancer. It was decided that Gary and I would go on our Mexican vacation as planned with our son and return home with one day in between only to have the lower lobe of my lung removed where the cancer had decided to harbor in my body one more time.

The amount of roller coaster emotions, high and lows that I have experienced in the past 12 months are almost more than can be imagined. I am confident that with the healing hand of the heavenly Father and the great surgeon I had that the cancer has been removed from my body and I am hopeful that more treatment will not be necessary.

I can tell you this – without the 3 "**Fs**" in my life, there is no way that I would have been able to survive 2014. My faith has been my rock and will continue to be my guide in all that I do. I know that there is an ultimate plan for each of our lives and our life destination is laid out for us in advance. My family has been there for me always. The grandchildren are my life. The innocence of them and their caring spirits is what keeps me going day after day. To be able to spend time with each one of them is a gift in itself. Each of my children and their spouses are definitely a gift from God. I anticipate the wedding of my youngest daughter Sara in April, which has been a highlight these past couple of months in some of my darkest moments. To be able to have the excitement of a wedding has truly been a blessing in disguise.

I am so fortunate to be able to have Gary by my side to help me when no one else can. Sometimes we take our spouses for granted. Being dependent with my last surgery has taught me not to take anyone for granted. And certainly, last but not least, my friends have been there through thick and thin.

Sometime we take life so for granted. My year of 2014 has taught me to take a step back, to stop and take a breath, and to slow down and remember what is really important in life. Three things are really important to me for 2015: **Faith**, **Family**, *and* **Friends**.

HERO OF HOPE

This closing story is about Linda Tobias, a leukemia cancer survivor who was presented with the Midwest Division Hero of Hope award at the 2014 Minnesota Leadership Conference held in Redwood Falls, Minnesota. The following quote is from the MURRAY COUNTY NEWS, November 19, 2014.

"...The Hero of Hope Award is presented annually to an outstanding survivor volunteer who exemplifies inspirational communication skills, passion for Relay For Life and the mission of the American Cancer Society, and commitment to eliminating cancer.

'The American Cancer Society is grateful for the generosity of those who share their story in order to help others understand how we are here to help families, friends, and community members when they need us most,' said Jennifer Evans, Specialist-Relay For Life. 'Linda (Tobias) does just that.'

'...The passion and energy (Linda) brings to Relay For Life inspires her fellow Relay members, offers hope, and encourages community involvement in the fight against cancer. Linda continually supports the mission of the American Cancer Society and emphasizes the need to continue our work to fight back through Relay.'

...Relay For Life is the world's largest movement to end cancer, where each year more than four million people in over 20 countries raise much-needed funds and awareness to save lives from cancer. To learn more about the American Cancer Society Relay for Life, visit RelayForLife.org or call 1-800-227-2345.

...The American Cancer Society is a global grassroots force of more than three million volunteers saving lives and fighting for every birthday threatened by every cancer in every community. As the largest voluntary health organization, the Society's efforts have contributed to a 20% decline in cancer death rates in the U.S. since 1991, and a 50% drop in smoking rates.

Thanks in part to our progress nearly 14 million Americans who have had cancer and countless more who have avoided it will celebrate more birthdays this year. As we marked our 100th birthday in 2013, we're determined to finish the fight against cancer. We're finding cures as the nation's largest private, not-for-profit investor in cancer research, ensuring people facing cancer have the help they need and continuing the fight for access to quality health care, life-saving screenings, clean air, and more. For more information, to get help or to join the fight, call us anytime, day or night, at 1-800-227-2345 or visit us at cancer.org."

The following is Linda's response at the Award ceremony.

"It is an honor to be here today and to be able to share with you. Relay For Life has been both inspirational and bitter sweet for me. When I think back to why I became involved with Relay 16 years ago it was because of the loss of my husband to colon cancer. It seemed like the right thing to do, I guess. When you lose someone to cancer, you are frustrated and you need to find some way to release those emotions so for me that way was to become involved with the Relay. How many of us have had that same experience? It was a coping mechanism for me in dealing with the loss of my husband. Did I know what I was really getting involved with? Probably not...

If you remember your first experience with Relay, it was probably a little overwhelming and yet exciting and yet we were so naïve because we had no idea what the big picture really was, did we?

This year we are celebrating 30 years of Relay For Life. Just think of the advances Relay has really achieved. Let me share something with you that I don't share very often...I am a Leukemia Cancer Survivor. When I was a young adult and just ready to being my life in the world, my parents were told I would never see my 25th birthday. I was sent to "I CAN COPE" classes to learn how to die with "dignity" instead of being set off to col-

lege...the "I CAN COPE" classes of the American Cancer Society of today are far different from the "I CAN COPE" classes that they had back in the 1970s...I went through the first class session with 8 people and everyone died in that class but me, and I was in my second class of 8 or 9 people, about half way through, and I said 'Enough of This!' and never went back. But keep in mind...that was before the days of Relay For Life – where they really began fighting for our lives. I am proud to say I just had my 59th birthday a couple of weeks ago...not that creeping up on 60 years is a good thing, but just think, guys...Relay For Life has made awesome strides in its 30 years. We have to be proud that we are making a difference. We should be shouting at the top of our lungs how awesome Relay is and what awesome strides have been made and what has been done to make differences in those people's lives that we care about...maybe even our own lives. You don't hear about "I CAN COPE" classes teaching you how to die with dignity anymore. You hear about all the American Cancer Survival Rates and creating a world with more birthdays and life expectancy and Survivors. The differences that have happened in the last 30 years are just phenomenal if you just think about it. Think of how many lives have been changed by Relay For Life.

In Murray County, just like in all your counties, we always get that same old question "What comes back to our county? What do we get for the money we give to Relay For Life?"

The answer my friends is quite simple if you are a cancer survivor or know a cancer survivor or if you raised money for the Relay For Life that made a difference for a cancer survivor. Then the answer is "THEY" come back and "THEY" make a difference. "THEY" make a difference to their families, to their friends, to their community and to society; to this whole world "THEY" make a difference in some way; "THEY" make a difference no matter how big or small; "THEY" make a difference to all of us. And I promise you this, I will continue to Relay as long as I can to support Relay to make this a better life for all of us in our communities and in our world. I challenge you to join me...together we can make a difference; we have made a huge difference; and we will continue to make a difference; and we will all "Create a world with more Birthdays" and "finish the fight for those we love and have loved." Thank you.

* * *

The preceding stories about cancer are not exactly in the scope of this book, but cancer touches almost everyone in one way or another. It is part of life, and if you noticed, the people in these stories came through their ordeals with a positive attitude. They allowed their Christian beliefs to guide them. It's part of life.

Chapter Six

Closure

THE GATES AND TRANSPARENCY

For almost the last three decades the United States has been at war with the Arab world. It started with the concern over possible nuclear weaponry production and chemical warfare buildup also. As it went on, we had the war almost won when President Obama came along. It would seem that his legacy will be that he lost the war and caused the dawning of ISIS, in addition to beginning the destruction of the United States as a Republic. My concern is this: if Hilary becomes the next President, will she finish the job he started?

It would seem that President Nixon didn't have it quite right in Watergate, but he taught the Democrats how to do it. Will we ever get to the truth about Whitewater Gate, Vince Foster Gate, ObamaCare Gate, Fast and Furious Gate, The Dept. of Internal Revenue Gate, the Benghazi Gate, and now the Hillary E-mail Gate? How many gates will there be before this is finished? Will the United States be beyond 30 or 40 trillion dollars in debt before we put a stop to all this? What will happen to our children?

JUST A NOTE FOR THE FUTURE

Why should we come together in the United States more like our Founding Fathers? Because we haven't been acting like them for some time now.

One very good reason would be because the United States is such a good alternative to tyranny. In fact, the United States is more than just a place in the world. The United States is a place in time itself. I think our past speaks for itself.

Although we have been subjected to forces which wanted to tear us apart, our basic structure is such that with our many freedom resolves, we have become almost impenetrable and indestructible. By that I mean our principles are impervious. The United States by rights has stood the test of time.

I am not saying we haven't had a few bad apples amongst us from time to time. But with all the world turmoil at the present, life almost any place else in the world is uncomfortable to some degree. The problems all seem to come from one faction or other, from deterioration and dishonesty. Why would we not want to change these issues for God's sake? How can there be any peace in the future if we continue on as we are doing?

I suppose we would do well if we brushed up on John Adam's and Benjamin Franklin's philosophies to shore up our future direction somewhat. For starters, possibly we could take our heads out of the sand and vote with a little more sanity, because Corruption breeds more Corruption.

The United States was built on the high ground, and I hope and pray the United States of America never loses sight of the Principles of our Founding Fathers.

CLOSURE

This book has been about the life span of any typical human being. Not all of us will reach old age. I realize that some will be taken early as God's will be done, or as our own foolish wishes or actions sometimes play out. At any rate, these words ring out as true as any ever spoken. They were given to me by an Intensive Care nurse, at the Longmont United Hospital in Colorado. She was one of several who were caring for me and others, when I had my heart attack. These words are appropriate for the closure of this book.

"GOD PROVIDES JUST WHAT YOU NEED, RIGHT WHEN YOU NEED IT. MAKE EVERY MOMENT COUNT, BECAUSE YOU NEVER KNOW WHEN YOUR LAST MOMENT WILL BE." ~Cori

Chapter Seven

Postscript

Although you might say this book is a recapitulation of life itself in general, it has the background of some eighty plus years of experience behind it.

The changes in life styles, politics, acceptable life attitudes, new inventions, and new laws all combine to change everything including how differently people act in these different environments. To put it in proper perspective, sixty years ago or more, people (in general) acted with more decency and higher moral values. Embezzlement (like the Enron case) just was NOT accepted or common. Life and liberty, people's rights, were not trampled on like they are today. Life was held sacred and more respected. Crime was less common and murder even less. Today the courts "plea bargain" most cases away and the only deterrent, the death penalty, has been subjected to so much unnecessary lawyer costs that it isn't used. We live in a time where the terms "clandestine", "mendacious", and "ludicrous" are the norm. Frankly, in my opinion, abortion and the death penalty should never have been legislated in the fashion to which they were, but more like in recent past, with less lawyer intrusion. In Washington's or Lincoln's time, many of today's judges would be considered totally unacceptable. Criminal sentencing today is inconsistent; time served for a crime does not equate or seem fitting. It seems that DNA evidence can be bought off with the claim of contamination. (Really, "contamination" is a million to one possibility, but the mere suggestion of it seems to work for the lawyers.) Money does talk and lawyers and judges seem to find ways to compromise the law for their own fame and fortune. I personally dislike striking this paradox between the existing now and yesteryear, but it had to be brought out in the open. We are going downhill.

In closing I leave you with one thought. What really happened to Vince Foster? Vince Foster was a brilliant lawyer, but he had one unusual character trait for a lawyer – he was a devout Christian. That may have worried other people around him. In the end, I find most people fear the truth itself more than anything else.

www.ingramcontent.com/pod-product-compliance
Lightning Source LLC
Chambersburg PA
CBHW060237050426
42448CB00009B/1487